S0-ABA-901

Dr. Linda Page's Healthy Healing Guide

Stress & Energy

Reduce Your Stress
&
Boost Your Energy

By
Linda Page, N.D., Ph.D.

Copyright ©1999 by Traditional Wisdom, Inc. All rights reserved. No part of this book may be used or reproduced in any manner whatsoever without the written permission of the Publisher. Printed in the United States of America.

Published by
Traditional Wisdom, Inc.
PO Box 436, Carmel Valley, CA 93924

ISBN: 1-884334-67-9 $9.95

Do you have natural health questions?
Call the Natural Health Information Service
1-900-903-5885, Monday through Friday,
9 AM to 5 PM Pacific Time.

Visit Dr. Linda Page
on the web: www.healthyhealing.com

If you have a problem finding the products
mentioned in this book, call
The Healthy House - 1-888-447-2939.

OTHER BOOKS BY
Linda Page, N.D., Ph.D.

Healthy Healing

Cooking For Healthy Healing

How To Be Your Own Herbal Pharmacist

Detoxification

Party Lights

(with restaurateur, Doug Vanderberg)

AND
The Healthy Healing Guide
& Library Book Series

Cancer
Fatigue Syndromes
Renewing Female Balance
Menopause & Osteoporosis
Sexuality
Fighting Infections With Herbs
Renewing Male Healthy & Energy

Weight Loss
Allergy Control
Anti-Aging
Do You Want To Have A Baby?
Colds & Flu
Detoxification & Body Cleansing
Boosting Immunity With Power Plants

Available in book stores, health food stores, and on the web: www.healthyhealing.com
For a free catalog, write to PO Box 436, Carmel Valley, CA   93924
For information about "Dr. Linda Page's Natural Healing Report," Call 1-800-408-0081.

Stress
is by far
the most common
health problem in the
world today

This small book is a
treasure chest.
It can help you cope in
a hundred ways with
daily stress — it can
help you transform
stress into creative
energy.

The information in this book is intended solely for information
and educational purposes, and not as medical advice.

Thanks to:

Kim Tunella - research and drafting.
Sarah Abernathy - editor, graphics and prepress project director.
Sylvia Zamora - assistant proofreader.
Barbara Howard - editor, cover design and director of marketing.
Deborah Warcken, marketing assistant.

Linda Page, N.D., Ph.D.

Long before natural foods and herbal formulas became a "chic," widely accepted method for healing, Dr. Linda Page was sharing her extensive knowledge with those who dared to listen.

During the late seventies, she opened and operated the Rainbow Kitchen, a natural food restaurant, and became a working partner in Sonora, California's Country Store, a natural foods store.

Through what some would call an accident of fate but she calls a blessing, she was compelled to research alternative avenues of healing. Sequestered in a hospital with a life-threatening illness, watching her 5-foot frame wither to 69 pounds, her hair drop out, and her skin peel off, doctors told her they had no cure. With only a cursory knowledge of herbs, she began a frantic research process of testing herbal formulas and healing food combinations on herself.

She read voraciously about herbal healing. Good friends shopped for herbs and she began to formulate the many compounds which would eventually save her life, revitalize her health and restore beautiful new hair and skin. It was that incident that led her to seek her degrees in Naturopathy and Nutrition.

A prolific author and educator, Dr. Page has sold over a million books including **Healthy Healing, Cooking For Healthy Healing, How To Be Your Own Herbal Pharmacist, Detoxification, Party Lights** and a popular series of library books which address specific healing therapies for topics like menopause, male and female energy, colds and flu, and cancer. Her book **Healthy Healing** is a textbook for courses at UCLA, The Institute of Educational Therapy, and Clayton College of Natural Health. Dr. Page also formulates over 250 herbal formulas for Crystal Star Herbal Nutrition of Earth City, Missouri. She received one of the first herbal patents in the United States for her formulas that help balance hormones to ease menopausal symptoms.

Dr. Page is an Adjunct Professor at Clayton College of Natural Health. She is also the executive editor of a monthly national natural health newsletter, *Dr. Linda Page's Natural Healing Report,* published by Weiss Research of Palm Beach Gardens, Florida.

Dr. Page appears weekly on a CBS television station with a report on natural healing; she is featured with CBS fitness reporter Bonnie Kaye on national CBS television; she is a principle speaker at national health symposiums and conventions; she is featured regularly in national magazines; she appears on hundreds of radio and television programs.

Today, Dr. Page delights in having come full circle. "I feel I am living my dream. I am so grateful that knowledge of healing through herbal formulas and good foods is becoming so widespread. I see it as an opportunity for people to seize the power to heal themselves. Knowledge is power. Whether one chooses conventional medicine, alternative healing avenues, or combines them both in a complementary process, the real prescription for healing is knowledge."

Coming Soon!

"You're The Doctor" Series
by
Linda Page, N.D., Ph.D.

Food Is Your Pharmacy™

Herbs Are Your Medicine™

Heal Yourself™

As affordable, high quality health care in America becomes more difficult to finance and obtain, natural therapies and personal wellness techniques are receiving more attention and favor. Over 75% of Americans now use some form of natural health care, from vitamins, to cleansing diets, to guided imagery, to herbal supplements.

Everyone needs more information about these methods to make informed choices for their own health and that of their families. The Healthy Healing Library Series was created to answer this need - with inexpensive, up-to-date books on the subjects people want to hear about the most.

The lifestyle therapy programs discussed in each book have been developed over the last fifteen years from the reported responses and successful healing results experienced by literally thousands of people. In addition, the full time research team at Healthy Healing Publications, Inc. investigates herbs, herbal combinations and herbal therapies from around the world for their availability and efficacy. You can feel every confidence that the recommendations are synthesized from real people with real problems who got real results.

Herbal medicines are highlighted in these books because they are in the forefront of modern science today. Herbal healing has the proven value of ancient wisdom and a safety record of centuries. Yet, science can only quantify, isolate, and assay to understand. Herbs respond to these methods, but they are so much more than the sum of their parts. God shows his face a little in herbs. They, too, have an ineffable quality.

Fortunately for us, our bodies know how to use herbs without our brains having to know why.

Table of Contents

Reduce Your Stress - Boost Your Energy

Stress is the universal enemy of modern mankind. As 21st century civilization races forward most Americans today are running harder and harder to stay in the same place. Experts tell us that a certain amount of stress is healthy, that facing challenges and difficulties helps us grow and reach our potential, even adding spice to our lives. But there's no doubt that excessive, prolonged stress drains our energy and creates an incredible load of body imbalances.

Many people seem to be under stress most of the time. New statistics reveal that over 20 million Americans have stress-related health problems! We try to get as much done as we can in as short a time as possible. Sometimes we try to do as many things as possible at the same time!

Financial obligations, kaleidoscopic job pressures, seeking work in an mercurial job market, family demands, emotional problems, health concerns, and lack of rest and leisure can overwhelm even the most stable, well-adjusted nature.

Stress is usually at the heart of heart disease. It is a major cause of chronic fatigue, insomnia, headaches, hypoglycemia, arthritis and compromised immunity. Degenerative diseases like cancers and diabetes are stress-related. Stress irritates body tissues in the form of gastritis, ulcers, cystitis, colitis and psoriasis. It irritates our mental processes in the form of moodiness, burn-out, overuse of drugs, depression and panic attacks. The common cold can be brought on by stress. Stress can even lead to baldness!

New statistics show that up to 95 percent of visits to health care professionals of all kinds are stress-related. If we can deal with stress first, other problems often improve automatically.

What exactly is stress?

I frequently hear people say that stress makes their body shrivel up and head for cover. Actually the opposite is true. Stress directly depletes the adrenal glands. Sufferers become less and less able to respond to stress and handle it. In prolonged cases, the adrenals cannot raise blood sugar when necessary and hypoglycemia results. In severe cases, like Addison's disease, the adrenals swell to the point of hemorrhage and tissue death may result.

Most of us know stress as the "fight or flight" concept — a basic response to perceived danger. But as stress has loomed larger in our lives, modern medical science has redefined stress more definitively. Today, there's specific and nonspecific stress, external and internal stress, emotional and biological stress, and physiological and environmental stress.

Can almost anything trigger a stress response? The number of recognized "stressors" is sweeping. Environmental disturbances like air pollution, plant pollens, toxic reactions to metals, or chemical halogens like chlorine and fluoride; physical trauma like infections, fractures, cuts, burns, parasite invasions, allergies, food sensitivities, or malnutrition (more common than one might think in America); even strong emotional reactions. Psychosocial stress, an umbrella covering almost every possible aspect of human life, is also recognized today. This doesn't count our personal, unique stressors. So, the answer is yes.... just about everything triggers stress.

What happens when the stress response is activated? Stress experts have identified three distinct stages as your body tries to adapt:

Stage 1: Alarm Reaction. This is the fabled "fight or flight" response. Your adrenal glands kick into action, releasing a flood of hormones that give you a burst of energy. Your heart rate and blood pressure increase. Your blood sugar levels rise as the liver releases stored sugar into your bloodstream. Your muscles tense; you start to sweat. Your immune system gets ready; blood-clotting mechanisms are enhanced. You're primed for quick action if needed. If the perceived danger passes, your alertness calms down and your pulse gradually returns to normal.

Stage 2: The Resistance Stage. Let's say your stress continues. Now your body starts to mobilize itself for a longer fight. The adrenal glands draw on nutrient reserves to provide longer-term energy by producing corticoid stress hormones to adapt to the stress. This mechanism works for a while, but if the stress continues, the nutrient and energy reserves are used up. Cell-damaging free radicals begin to form in greater numbers; the adrenal glands, cardiovascular and immune response systems become exhausted from holding up a constant state of arousal.

Stage 3: The Exhaustion Stage. If your stress is unrelenting, your body's nutrient and energy reserves become even more depleted. With nothing more to draw on, your adrenal glands fall into a state of exhaustion, perpetually releasing the hormones adrenaline, noradrenaline and cortisol, a futile coping effort that drastically diminishes your body's ability to deal with any stress at all. Adrenal exhaustion affects all body systems and places a great load on our organ systems, especially the heart, blood vessels, pancreas (hypoglycemia is a common result), and leads to other gland malfunction, like low sexual energy. If your diet is also poor, your body's nutritional storehouse will have almost no raw materials to draw on for normalizing itself, and serious damage may take place to your kidneys, liver, gastrointestinal tract, bones and immune system. You can easily see how serious stress can become.

Can your body cope with stress? Can you transform stress into spice?

Fortunately, the stress process can be turned around. We can dramatically strengthen our body's ability to adapt to stress so that it doesn't undermine our physical and mental health. It's the extremes that get us into trouble.... when stress is unusual or long-lasting. Typically, the stress response is a mild and managable experience because the human body is designed to handle normal stressful situations.

Further, the same stress that can make one person sick can be an invigorating experience for another. The goal isn't to avoid all stress, but to maintain a high degree of health and survive stress well. Controlling chronic stress may require reorganization of your lifestyle. Major problems usually require major change.

The key is to give your body the tools to respond to stress. Poor health cannot be blamed entirely on stress. We fall prey to stress because of poor health. A balanced approach combining nutrition, exercise, and relaxation techniques can give your mind and body the tools it needs to successfully deal with stress.

You're the doctor. You can transform stress into spice. Here's my lifestyle program to improve the quality of your life.

Food is your Pharmacy™ for relieving stress.

—Believe it or not, your diet is your key to a stress free life. Adrenal health is critical. If your adrenal glands are exhausted, they need nourishment, or you'll never recover your energy. Only a good diet can feed them.

—During periods of intense stress your body needs a lot more nutrients. A nourishing diet stops emergency borrowing by your body of protein, minerals, vitamins and fats to cope with extra stress. Even when certain nutrients are drawn down to give you bursts of extra energy, they can be restored quickly.

—How you eat may be as important as what you eat because it affects how you metabolize your food. Eat in a relaxing environment, not when you're upset, distracted or on the run.

—Do you eat foods high in calories, sugar and fat to get quick energy when you're under stress. Today, most of these foods are also full of chemicals and heavily refined. They degrade your bio-chemical balance and actually elevate stress.

—Do you use caffeine to boost your energy, or alcohol to relax your stress? Caffeine increases stress symptoms of nervousness, irritability, headaches and heart palpitations. Alcohol escalates your adrenal hormone output, interfering with sleep cycles and normal brain chemistry.

—Protein is critical in a stress reduction diet. Extreme, unyielding stress uses up a lot of protein. Adding clean protein from seafoods, sea plants, rice, sprouts, soy foods, nuts, seeds, organic turkey and chicken, eggs and low fat cheeses helps stop stress-related tissue destruction. Amino acids in protein foods help build healthy neurotransmitters which affect mood and mechanisms for coping with stress. For example, the amino acid L-tryptophan (in soy, cheeses and turkey) helps build serotonin, essential for overcoming anxiety, depression and insomnia.

Here's my step-by-step Anti-Stress Diet:

Begin with a 2 day liquid diet to clear your body of chemicals and pollutants that aggravate stress. Follow with 1 to 2 days of all-fresh foods to rebalance your body's chemistry (pH). Add plenty of supergreen foods like chlorella, barley grass, green kamut, etc. for molecular proteins and chlorophyllins that can be absorbed directly into cell membranes to start rebuilding your body and give you energy. Then add whole grains root vegetables and potatoes to boost serotonin for more emotional stability. Then add protein foods (see above) to help you think and react quickly and feel more energetic.

—On rising: take a glass of 2 fresh squeezed lemons, 1 TB. maple syrup and 8-oz. of water.

—Breakfast: (1st day) have a nutrient-dense Kick-Off Cleansing Cocktail: juice 1 handful fresh wheat grass or parsley—extremely rich in chlorophyll and antioxidants, 4 carrots, 1 apple, 2 celery stalks with leaves, $\frac{1}{2}$ beet with top. (Days 2-4), add a whole grain cereal with yogurt or apple juice on top; brown rice with sea veggies on top;, or a poached egg.

—Mid-morning: have a glass of fresh carrot juice or fresh apple juice. Add 1 TB. of a green superfood like Crystal Star ENERGY GREEN™ drink mix or Vibrant Health GREEN VIBRANCE.

—Lunch: (1st day) have a Salad-In-A-Glass: juice 4 parsley sprigs, 3 quartered tomatoes, $\frac{1}{2}$ green or red pepper, $\frac{1}{2}$ cucumber, 1 scallion, 1 lemon wedge. (Days 2-4) add brown rice and steamed vegetables or baked tofu, or a fresh green salad with cottage cheese and bottled water.

—Mid-afternoon: have a cup of chamomile or green tea and celery stick with kefir cheese.

—Dinner: (1st day) have a warm, mineral electrolyte broth: for two bowls: chop and cover with water in a soup pot, 4 carrots, 2 potatoes with skins, 1 onion, 3 stalks celery with leaves, 2 broccoli stalks, $\frac{1}{2}$ head cabbage and 1 handful fresh parsley. Simmer covered 30 minutes; strain, discard solids and drink liquid. (Days 2-4) Add a sea food dish, cous-cous or brown rice or a whole grain pasta with a light cheese sauce. And have Super Soup, with antioxidants and immune boosters: for two bowls: chop and cover with water in a soup pot, 1 cup broccoli, 1 leek (white parts), 2 cups peas, $\frac{1}{2}$ cup scallions, 4 cups chard leaves, $\frac{1}{2}$ cup fennel bulb, $\frac{1}{2}$ cup fresh parsley, 6 garlic cloves, 2 tsp. astragalus extract (or $\frac{1}{4}$ cup pieces astragalus bark), 6 cups vegetable stock, a pinch cayenne, 1 cup green cabbage, $\frac{1}{4}$ cup sea vegetables. Bring ingredients to a boil, simmer 10 min. Let sit 20 minutes.

What's water got to do with stress? Don't forget water in your anti-stress program.

Low water intake leads to dehydration. Dehydration contributes to stress because brain functions that depend on electrical energy in the brain become less efficient. Stress causes the mobilization of primary nutrients and water from body reserves. Basically, dehydration causes stress and stress causes further dehydration. Drink 8 -10 glasses (8-oz) of water every day.

Herbs are superior body balancers for boosting energy and releasing stress.

Herbs are rich in replacement minerals, trace minerals, and plant enzymes. They provide inner strength with bio-active amino acids and electrolytes that help restore body and mind energy. They correct nutrient deficiencies with B complex vitamins, vitamin C and bioflavonoids that fortify you when the going gets tough. Sometimes you can even expect miracles.

Adrenal exhaustion can keep you locked in a low-energy/high-stress loop. Herbs are some of the best therapy I know for revitalizing swollen, exhausted adrenal glands.

Are your adrenals exhausted? Three or more yes answers should alert you.
—Do you lack energy or alertness and have a poor memory?
—Do you have severely cracked, painful heels?
—Do you have nervous moistness of hands and soles of feet?
—Do you have brittle, peeling nails or extremely dry skin?
—Do you have frequent heart palpitations or panic attacks?
—Do you have chronic heartburn and poor digestion?
—Do you have chronic lower back pain (adrenal swelling)?
—Do you have hypoglycemia and cravings for salt or sweets?
—Do you have unexplained moodiness, crying spells and guilt?
—Do you have extreme sensitivity to odors, or certain foods?
—Do you have high incidence of yeast or fungal infections?

You can also test yourself for adrenal exhaustion: Here's a common diagnostic performed by chiropractors, massage therapists and naturopaths with a home blood pressure testing kit:

1. Lie down and rest for 5 minutes. Take a blood pressure reading. Your systolic blood pressure should be below 120 and your diastolic blood pressure should be below 80 for health.

2. Stand up and immediately take another blood pressure reading. If your blood pressure drops below normal levels, your adrenals are probably functioning poorly. The amount of drop is usually in ratio to the amount of adrenal dysfunction.

To activate and nourish adrenals, I use herbs like *licorice, sarsaparilla* and *Siberian ginseng* which work specifically to stimulate adrenal glands. Try Crystal Star ADRN-ACTIVE™ (with *licorice root, sarsaparilla, bladderwrack, uva ursi, Irish moss, ginger, astragalus root, capsicum and rosehips*).

—High quality royal jelly is another excellent choice. I've taken 1 teasp. every day for years. Royal jelly is a rich source of pantothenic acid for healthy adrenals.

Two other types of Herbs are your Medicine™ for conquering stress.

Adaptogens are herbs that help your body adapt to stressful situations because they work to restore balance. Adaptogenic herbs are primary support for adrenal function, so they're very effective in preventing stress-related ailments while increasing stamina and endurance.

—Ginsengs of all kinds, for example, are some of Nature's most powerful adaptogens. They are potent adrenal tonics and quickly enhance the body's response to stress, increasing mental performance and restoring normal vitality. Their anti-anxiety effects are comparable to those of Valium. Ginsengs do even more toward preventing future stress illnesses. They offset some of the negative effects of cortisone, enhance liver function and protect against radiation damage. Best results when using ginsengs for anti-stress effects, including *panax and American ginseng* (2gr. 3x daily), *Siberian ginseng, ashwagandha, suma and dong quai* (3gr. 3x daily), are obtained over a period of 2 to 3 weeks, followed by a 1 to 2 week rest period. This pattern of using ginseng, resting, using ginseng, etc. appears to work best for the adrenal glands.

Nervines are herbs that rejuvenate and restore the nerve system from the damages of stress.

—Sedative nervines like *valerian, hops, kava kava, and lavender* reduce anxiety, calm the nerves and help you sleep.

—Analgesic nervines like *valerian, chamomile or St. John's wort* reduce nerve or muscle pain.

—Soporific nervines like *valerian, catnip and hops* encourage deeper, more refreshing sleep.

—Tonic nervines like *sea vegetables, wild oats, celery and passionflowers* nourish the nervous system and can be taken for extended periods of time (three months or more).

• Valerian root is one of Nature's safest, most effective tranquilizers with a remarkable effect on the brain and nervous system. Studies show sleep-inducing, muscle-relaxing effects. Valerian's electrolyte minerals and copper nutritionally support nerve tissue. I have used VALERIAN-HOPS FORMULA, (a Rosemary Gladstar formula), and Flora Labs FLORASED VALERIAN to good effect.

• Kava Kava is a natural anti-anxiety, sedative herb, with active kavalactones that make it a safe replacement for benzodiazepines or tranquilizers in treating anxiety, insomnia, restlessness and memory loss. Both Jarrow Formulas KAVA CAPS and Gaia KAVA KAVA EXTRACT are effective.

Beyond these principle single herbs, herbal combinations work even better for a broad spectrum of stress-related reactions. A good compound will have herbs that help repair damaged nerve sheathing, herbs that quiet the brain without addictive side effects, herbs that help stabilize body balance and emotions. Many combination work quite rapidly, often within 30 minutes. Crystal Star Relax Caps™ is highly effective (with *ashwagandha, black cohosh, scullcap, kava kava, black haw, hops, valerian, European mistletoe, wood betony, lobelia and oatstraw*).

For a nice mental pick-me-up to combat stress headaches, nervousness and afternoon let-down fatigue, try Crystal Star Relax™ Tea.

If you plan to add vitamins to your "less stress, more energy" program.....

I believe fresh, unsprayed, organically grown food, along with herbs and super foods like chlorella, spirulina, wheat grass, barley grass, bee pollen and sea vegetables, are the best choice for fighting stress and boosting energy. These foods have a full spectrum of nutrients vastly superior to partitioned, man-made vitamin, mineral or other isolated nutrients.

The nutrients in living foods are organized into extremely subtle and complex patterns that cannot be duplicated except in a living environment. In my experience, their vitamins, minerals, and other nutrients are immeasurably more effective for healing. If you plan to use vitamin and mineral supplements to enhance the nutritional vitality in your diet, I recommend those that are derived from natural substances or food-grown.

—Adrenal gland health is critical for stress relief and more energy. Key adrenal nutrients like vitamin C, B-5 (pantothenic acid), vitamin B-6, zinc and magnesium are depleted during stressful times. Consider the following daily dosages: vitamin C up to 3,000mg, pantothenic acid 500mg, B-6,100mg, zinc 30mg, magnesium 500mg to overcome chronic stress.

—B vitamins supercharge us physically and emotionally. They can enhance our thinking and help boost our morale. Yet B vitamins are so meagerly supplied in the Standard American Diet that most people lack them. If you are tired, nervous, irritable, or depressed, suspect a vitamin B deficiency. I like dietary sources best, but if you're under a lot of stress, consider 100mg B-complex supplement daily (food grown if possible). B vitamins work together and should be taken together, but the B-vitamins involved in stress relief are B-1, B-5, B-6, and B-12.

B-1 (thiamine) helps your body convert glucose into energy. Your body needs more of it during times of stress. B-1 is depleted by eating refined sugar. Food sources: brown rice, eggs, peas and beans, rice, wheat germ, brewer's yeast, fish, poultry and liver.

B-5 (pantothenic acid) is called the anti-stress vitamin. Short term B-5 deficiency can cause wear and tear on the adrenal glands; long term deficiency may cause unreversable damage. Food sources: whole grains, legumes, brewer's yeast, cauliflower, broccoli, sweet potatoes, eggs, beef, mushrooms, nuts, royal jelly, whole rye flour, salmon, saltwater fish, and liver.

B-6 (pyridoxine) is required for the release of glycogen for energy from the liver and muscles and for the absorption of B-12. Food sources: brewer's yeast, carrots, peas, spinach, sunflower seeds, walnuts, wheat germ, eggs, fish and meat.

B-12 (cyanocobalamin) prevents anemia fatigue. Food sources: brewer's yeast, sea vegetables (such as dulse, kelp, kombu and nori), soybeans, eggs, dairy, herring, mackerel, sea food, kidney, liver and herbs like alfalfa and hops.

Antioxidant vitamins are specific for good stress response. I recommend three:

—Vitamin C complex - Your body excretes more vitamin C when it's under stress. You need extra amounts of this antioxidant to help support your immune system during stress. A serious deficiency of vitamin C causes a sharp reduction of hormone production by the adrenal glands. Food sources: berries, citrus fruits, kiwi, melons, green leafy veggies, asparagus, avocados, broccoli, peas, sea veggies, onions, papayas, pineapple and strawberries. Use a vitamin C complex with bioflavonoids (like hesperidin, rutin, and quercetin) to help the adrenals better cope with stress. Sonne's Organic Foods Natural Source Vitamin C.

—Vitamin E, another strong antioxidant, maintains healthy nerves against stress. Food sources: vegetable oils, soy foods, nuts, seeds, green leafy vegetables and wheat germ.

—Alpha-lipoic acid potentiates the benefits of both vitamin C and E and adds its own powerful antioxidant effects. (Water-soluble vitamin C reaches the watery parts of cells; fat soluble vitamin E works with the fatty parts of cells; alpha-lipoic acid is both water and fat soluble moving into all parts of the cell to neutralize free radicals.) Supplementation is best as a therapeutic.

Look to your diet for more minerals if you're under stress. Important stress-relieving minerals calcium, magnesium, potassium and zinc nourish your nerves. Here's how:

—Calcium helps maintain normal heartbeat and nerve impulses. If your calcium is low you might be noticing heart palpitations, nervousness, reduced ability to think clearly, insomnia and depression. Food sources: green leafy vegetables, almonds, asparagus, molasses, brewer's yeast, broccoli, cabbage, sea veggies, figs, oats, prunes, sesame seeds, tofu, watercress and dandelion greens, carob, yogurt, dairy foods and seafood.

—Magnesium plays an essential role in the transmission of nerve and muscle impulses which causes irritability and nervousness. If your magnesium is low you might be noticing insomnia, mental spaciness, irritability, rapid heartbeat, anxiety or chronic tiredness. Food sources: green leafy vegetables, apples, apricots, avocados, bananas, molasses, brewer's yeast, brown rice, cantaloupe, sea veggies, figs, garlic, citrus fruits, lima beans, nuts, peaches, sesame seeds, soybeans, watercress and dandelion greens, whole grains, dairy foods, salmon, and seafood.

—Potassium is critical for healthy nerves and a regular heart beat. Potassium deficiency shows up as cognitive impairment, nervousness, insomnia, periodic headaches and depression. Food sources: dried fruit, avocados, bananas, blackstrap molasses, brewer's yeast, brown rice, dulse, garlic, nuts, potatoes, winter squash and yams.

—Zinc is needed for protein synthesis, critical to your body's ability to deal with stress (pg. 9). If your zinc is low you may be noticing unusual fatigue, memory impairment or increased susceptibility to infections and acne. Food sources: brewer's yeast, seafoods and sea veggies, eggs, pumpkin seeds, soy lecithin, sunflower seeds and whole grains.

Probiotics (friendly bacteria) reduce stress, too.

Stress clearly upsets the delicate balance of friendly flora in your gastrointestinal tract. Friendly bacteria perform essential tasks for maintaining high energy. They also synthesize B-vitamins for keeping stress responses normal. Low friendly bacteria means that unfriendly inhabitants like *candida albicans and E. coli* can take over. Products I've used effectively include Professional Nutrition Doctor-DophilUs+Fos, Transformation Enzyme Plantadophilus, Wakunaga Kyo-Dophilus, Nature's Path, Flora-Lyte, Jarrow Formulas Jarro-Dophilus+Fos, Prevail Inner Ecology.

Ten stress relieving techniques the experts advise:

1: Get a little perspective. Overreacting, taking things too personally, letting "things" rule your life, are guaranteed stressors. Develop a sense of humor about life's little surprises — see them as an opportunity instead of a curse.

2: Learn to manage your own time better. Delegate more, say no when demands from others or yourself aren't realistic.

3: Take a short get-away vacation. Even a week-end in the beauty of nature can do wonders to change outlook, emotions and body chemistry. You have to unwind before you can unleash.

4: Take an alternating hot and cold shower to stimulate circulation and clear your head. It's never-fail stress relief for me; you might be surprised at how your attitude and mood will change.

5: A massage, full or partial, even self-given, stimulates oxygen uptake and blood flow.

6: Meditation is clinically proven for stress relief. Some experts call it a massage for the mind. While formal transcendental meditation takes practice, almost anything that calms you, and takes you away from stress can be a "meditation."

I often recommend gardening, a crossword puzzle, a good mystery story — even an hour's walk can remove your mind from a stressful situation and bring stillness to chaotic thoughts.

7: A little help from your friends. Just by listening, friends can help you get through tough times. Nourish your friendships. People with supporting friends handle stress much better than those who rely only on themselves.

8: Fresh air exercise 3 to 4 days a week, increases nutrient uptake, tissue oxygen levels and body balance. Exercise reduces muscle tension as much as 25%, and reduces anxiety for up to 2 hours after an exercise session. Exercise also reduces fatigue, mental tension and depression.

9: Diaphragmatic breathing, (like taking a deep breath before a hard task) is especially good for mental equilibrium. Breathing from your diaphragm helps you relax almost instantly.

Follow this deep breathing tip: Begin by putting your hand on your abdomen just below the navel. Inhale slowly through your nose and watch your hand move out as your belly expands. Hold the breath for a few seconds, then exhale slowly. Repeat several times.

10: Get early morning sunlight on your body every day possible. Sunlight increases the blood's capacity to carry oxygen and deliver it to the tissues. Sunlight also increases your feeling of well-being, has relaxing effects and helps you sleep better.

New research shows that short exposures to sunlight can increase your tolerance to stress by heightening cell energy levels and boosting your endurance. Sunlight also relaxes your breathing and heart rate, and helps reduce blood sugar and blood pressure.

Men and Women Respond Differently to Stress

Men and women are on the same planet, but hardly anything else is the same. Many things that stress men don't affect women and vice versa. I can say beyond a shadow of a doubt that men and women have different stress and fatigue "triggers." Even in similar stress situations men and women react differently and cope differently.

Programs to help treat men's and women's stress reactions are also very different. After many years of intensive work, I've developed effective, all-natural healing pathways for men and women to handle their stress.

What stresses out men? Men want to feel on top of things, in control, so finances, work and doubt (about themselves or anything else) are the biggest stressors for men.

How do men react to these stressors? First, they tend to hold stress in, to bottle it up. They remain stoic or have grim reactions.

But when men finally express their stress, it's much more actively than women - usually through anger or shouting, sometimes violence. Still, men are becoming more aware of these tendencies. Today, I know a lot of men who look to natural solutions to relax and cope.

What are the best stress busters, the biggest energy returners for men?
A high energy diet for men is the best place to start.
1: Get the junk food out of your life. Men know it isn't the best for their health, but I've heard a lot of men say that junk food is comfort food for them. They tend to overeat it, but believe me, comforting or not, it's still fried, fatty and fast.
   Overeating any foods can drain energy. Overeating junk food puts additional stress on your liver. It slows down your metabolism because it requires an enormous amount of energy for digestion. For more male energy and less stress, eat smaller meals more frequently, with a focus on more low fat, high fiber foods. It's the best choice.... and is also good for a man's heart.
   One of my favorite choices for men, especially if their energy drops mid-afternoon and they're tempted to binge, is a green drink, with high chlorophyll superfoods. Alfalfa, wheat grass and spirulina transport oxygen to the cells to restore energy and help cut through fatty waste that slows a man's body down. Men tell me a green drink carries them through an afternoon just fine. They're easy and convenient to take in the single size serving for a pick-me-up.

2: Drink more WATER. Chronic dehydration is a common cause of low energy. Other groups of foods that men tend to overdo, like caffeine and sugary sodas, dehydrate the system.

3: Get plenty of high quality PROTEIN.... very important for a man's energy needs. Men need denser foods than women. But protein doesn't have to come from meats or dairy foods. Protein from seafoods rich in Omega-3 oils help energize a man, *and* protect his heart and prostate. Beans and peas, dark greens, cruciferous vegetables and soy foods offer healthy vegetarian protein to keep a man energized.

4: Add ANTIOXIDANT-RICH FOODS like citrus fruits, vegetables, garlic and organic grapes to fight free radicals. Free radical damage exhausts a man's energy and sets the stage for more serious problems like cancer and heart disease if left unchecked later in life.

5: Eat ZINC-RICH FOODS to restore hormonal balance and recharge sex drive — especially from seafood like crab, lobster and oysters. Organic turkey, sunflower and pumpkin seeds, eggs, mushrooms, brewer's yeast and wheat germ are other good zinc sources.

6: Eat more fresh foods for ENZYME THERAPY to improve digestive disorders like heartburn- a big stress problem for men. Fresh food enzymes help speed up digestion and energize.

7: LOVE YOUR LIVER - Low energy is the one of the first signs of liver congestion, a common man's problem.

Do you have a sluggish liver? Here are the signs:
—Are you tired a lot with no explained reason?
—Do you crave alcohol and sugar excessively?
—Do you have a distended stomach even if the rest of your body is thin? (A man who is thin everywhere else, but who has a protruding stomach often has a stress swollen liver.)
—Do you have cellulitic "love handles" on your torso even if you are thin?
—Do you feel mentally confused or spaced out?
—Are your bowel movements sluggish? Or alternating between constipation and diarrhea?
—Do you have extremely poor digestion?
—Do you get frequent unexplained headaches and have bags under your eyes?
—Do you have gallstones or kidney stone attacks?
—Do you have a yellowish tint to your skin, liver spots on the skin, or spots before your eyes? (Your liver may be eliminating toxins through different body avenues.
—Do you have poor hair texture or unusually slow hair growth? (Your liver may not be using fat soluble vitamins properly.)
—Do you have chronic skin itching or chronic peeling on your palms or the soles of your feet?

Here's my healthy healing, tried and true, short liver cleanse for energy:

The night before your liver cleanse.....
—Take a cup of miso soup with sea veggies snipped on top.

The next day....
—On rising: I lemon squeezed, or 2 TBS. lemon juice in water; or 2 TBS. cider vinegar in water with I teasp. honey.
—Breakfast: a glass of carrot/beet/cucumber juice, or apple juice. Add I teasp. spirulina.
—Mid-morning: a green veggie drink; boost it with a green super food powder mixed in (look for ones with barley and alfalfa sprouts, chlorella, spirulina and sea veggies like dulse).
—Lunch: a glass of fresh carrot juice or apple juice.

—Mid-afternoon: a cup of peppermint tea or another green drink.
—Dinner: another carrot juice or a hot vegetable broth
—Bedtime: pineapple/papaya juice with 1 teasp. honey or royal jelly.

Add some herbs to your cleanse. Many herbs are highly effective liver tonics that cleanse the liver and re-establish body chemistry. Look for a liver tea like Crystal Star Liv-Alive™ Tea (with *dandelion, yellow dock, hyssop, watercress, milk thistle seed, red sage, pau d'arco, Oregon grape, licorice rt., parsley and hibiscus)* and use for 1 month for best results.

For long term liver support, add a 1 to 3 month course of Milk Thistle Seed Extract drops.

Beyond food choices, here are some more male energizers to overcome stress:

Hormone energizers can pull an older man out of an energy slump! It hasn't been well-publicized, but men, like women, have hormonal cycles that influence their physical and mental performance. Testosterone levels, critical to male energy, can fluctuate dramatically (between 250 to 1,200 nanograms) at different times in a man's life. Testosterone levels start declining around age 40, falling about 10% each decade.

This phenomenon is called male "andropause" and can lead to decreased sex drive and loss of strength and energy for a man. Herbal hormone energizers like panax ginseng, sarsaparilla and saw palmetto nourish the male reproductive system, encourage testosterone balance and help pull an older man out of an energy slump.
Here are two of my favorite recommendations that work fast:

Crystal Star Super Man's Energy™ Extract (with *sarsaparilla rt., saw palmetto, suma, Siberian ginseng, gotu kola and capsicum*).

Crystal Star Male Ginsiac™ Extract with potency wood (contains *fresh American panax ginseng, damiana, ginkgo biloba, potency wood, gotu kola, saw palmetto, ginger and capsicum.*)

Exercise is an energy key for men. The best stress releasing therapies for men are physical. Take a hike, run, play a little football. Exercise lowers stress hormones and increases your body's feel-good, pain relieving endorphins. Exercise improves a man's sleep and sex drive, protects against his heart disease and Alzheimer's and even promotes a longer life.

Add Siberian Ginseng Extract during your workout for best results. It's a premier adaptogen and energizer that can boost a man's work performance and workout endurance.

Finally, since a man's stress is physically expressed, muscle relaxants are always important. Herbs like scullcap, black cohosh and kava kava ease muscle stress and improve sleep. Kava kava has been in the news for its sedative effects but here's what you may not know: Key kava active components go directly to muscle tissue to reduce painful contractions. And, kava calms the mind without causing over-sedation like Valium.

Try Crystal Star Stressed Out Extract (with *black cohosh, scullcap, black haw, wood betony, kava kava and carrot.*) Most men feel the effects in 15 to 20 minutes!

What stresses out women? Relationships, family and married life, and feeling out of control are the biggest stressors for women.

How do women react to these stresses? Women tend to worry, cry or become extremely anxious. Women are a bigger target for depression than men, largely because they don't feel as much in control of their lives as men.... a reaction that leads to depression. Just like men, though, women are tired. Four out of 5 women place persistent fatigue among their "top 10" health concerns.

Why are women so tired? Most health professionals agree that hormone fluctuations, exhausted adrenals, and thyroid problems are the biggest energy zappers for women today.

What are the best stress busters, the biggest energy returners for women?
    A high energy diet focused on organic, hormone-balancing foods is the place to start.
    1: Reduce HIGH FAT DAIRY PRODUCTS and meats that are notoriously high in added hormones. Hormones, especially estrogens, disrupt a woman's body balance. Eat organic foods whenever you can.

    2: Eat CRUCIFEROUS VEGGIES like broccoli and cauliflower to help flush excess estrogen from pollutants out of your body.

    3: Reduce sugar and caffeine. Both foods drain the adrenal glands — responsible for energy!

    4: Include B-VITAMIN FOODS like brown rice (mental energy and stress support), magnesium-rich foods like leafy greens (blood sugar regulating and heart/muscle support), iron-rich foods like peas, molasses and leafy greens (healthy blood).

    5: Most of all, EAT FOODS FROM THE SEA to restore female vitality.
    —Add sea vegetables to your ongoing diet. Sea vegetables act as total body tonics to restore female vitality, especially during menopause. Sea vegetables are a rich source of fat-soluble vitamins like D and K which help women's bodies make steroidal hormones like estrogen and DHEA to support her during menopause. They are also high in bone building minerals, anti-stress protein and alginic acid which binds to and eliminates toxins from the body. Just 2 TBS. a day are therapy. And it's so easy. Just snip dried sea plants like nori, wakame, dulse, kombu and kelp onto anything you like... rice, pizza, salad, soups, anything.
    —Have cold water fish or seafood 2 to 3 times a week for EFAs, vital to hormone balance, nervous system health and mental energy. Salmon is one of God's gifts, a rich source of Omega-3 fatty acids and vitamin E. (Salmon is farm-raised now so you don't have to worry about endangerment as we do with swordfish).

    6: Balance your hormones with herbs. Herbal hormone energizers work extremely well for women. HORMONAL FLUCTUATIONS often cause tiredness and irritability. After menopause many women find their energy levels at an all-time low as hormone production slows down.

Herbs like *ashwagandha, dong quai* and *damiana* can restore a woman's hormone harmony and a waning libido. Combined together, the herbs can even relieve serious chronic fatigue syndromes. Crystal Star FEM-SUPPORT™ EXTRACT (*ashwagandha, dong quai and damiana*) has been my own choice when needed.

7: **Is your thyroid sluggish?** Low thyroid affects millions of unsuspecting women. It's linked to many stress reactions - depression, anxiety and fatigue. The thyroid gland produces hormones which keep metabolic rates normal - especially the balance of hormones such as estrogen and progesterone. It stabilizes energy-producing and energy-using processes.

If your thyroid isn't working the way you'd like (you're probably noticing some recent, unexplained weight gain), natural iodine herbal supplements are the best thing I know to help you normalize thyroid activity.

Iodine and mineral-rich herbs also help regulate metabolism. Minerals activate digestion to keep food available for fuel and energy. A thyroid support herbal enhances kidney, gallbladder and pancreatic functions, promoting vitality as it encourages a lazy thyroid. Because thyroid health is so primary to metabolic activity, many people use thyroid support herbs as part of a weight control program to help reduce the "middle age spread."

Check these body signs if you think your thyroid is low:
—Are you unusually fatigued (especially in the morning)?
—Do you have swollen ankles, hands or eyelids?
—Do you have chronic bloating, gas and indigestion?
—Have you lost head hair and gained facial hair?
   especially after menopause?
—Have you gained weight for no explained reason?
—Have you recently noticed breast thickenings or fibroids?
—Are you unusually depressed or anxious (poor immune response)?

You can test thyroid function at home. All you need is a basal thermometer.

Place a basal thermometer under your arm for ten minutes before getting out of bed in the morning. The thermometer must read to tenths of a degree. Normal body temperature ranges for this test are between 97.8 and 98.2 degrees Fahrenheit.

A reading below 97.8 may indicate hypothyroid activity (low thyroid); a reading above may indicate hyperthyroid activity (excess thyroid).

Some low thyroid problems can be treated without thyroid drugs. I use sea vegetables to activate an underactive thyroid. They are ideal for thyroid balancing. As a rich source of organic iodine, sea veggies can shore up iodine deficiencies (regularly involved with thyroid problems) and boost energy and metabolism.

Crystal Star META-TABS ACTIVE™ (with *parsley, kelp, Irish moss, sarsaparila, watercress, mullein, lobelia and carrot*) is a good choice for thyroid balancing.

A thyroid-tyrosine glandular product is another good choice to normalize thyroid health and improve energy levels. I recommend Enzymatic THYROID-TYROSINE CAPS.

Here are some female herbal energizers to help overcome stress:

Restoring mental energy is important for women's stress reduction. *Gotu kola*, a ginseng-like herb, is a favorite of mine for women because it provides energy, nourishes her brain and also restores her nerves. Taking *gotu kola* in a combination with other mental energy herbs is an even better choice. Crystal Star MENTAL INNER ENERGY™ (with *kava kava, Chinese, American and Siberian ginseng, dong quai, suma, fo-ti, gotu kola, ginkgo biloba and ashwagandha*).

A woman can rewire her nervous system with herbs. A formula like Crystal Star RELAX CAPS™ (with *ashwagandha, black cohosh, scullcap, kava kava, black haw, hops, valerian, European mistletoe, wood betony, lobelia and oatstraw*) can rebuild the nerve sheath, reduce mood swings and encourage deep sleep. Most women feel less stressed within 25 minutes.

Deep breathing is an essential stress reducer-energy builder for women. Deep breathing for just one minute tones your entire body, increases body oxygen and relieves fatigue.

It also reduces hot flashes in menopausal women. A study from Wayne State University shows that hot flashes can be decreased by 50% just by slow, deep breathing!

Breathe in deeply through your nose from your belly — your stomach should flatten slightly and your chest should puff up. Breathe out completely through your mouth. Repeat 10 times for best results.

Women hold stress in their bodies. They are less likely than a man to release it physically. Stretch out.... in the morning and before you retire. The neck, shoulders, low back and abdomen are stress targets. Stretching reduces muscular stress and increases flexibility. Stretching also guards against low back pain, a common problem for women today.

Yoga is a good option for women. Yoga postures help realign the body and allow energy to flow more freely. In addition, yoga settles and stabilizes a jangly mind.

Finally, if you're one of today's "superwomen," the best medicine is often getting enough rest. Going a mile a minute every day can lead to a burn-out energy crash.

Has Stress Turned Into Depression For You?

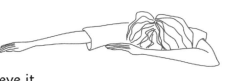

Chronic depression is a stress reaction that disrupts the lives of more than 30 million Americans. It's both a mental and emotional state and over twenty-eight million Americans take antidepressant drugs or anxiety medications to relieve it.

Psychologists tell us that mild depression may actually be a natural phenomenon of growth and progress in our lives. Falling to the depths of depression and climbing back out can force us into character-building (the old "you can't make an omelet without breaking eggs" theory). Coping with hardships, relationship problems and thorny negative feelings is part of the process of life. For most people, it's a state that passes as the individual's outlook climbs upward. For people who can't climb out, understanding the nature and causes of their depression offers a powerful tool for overcoming it.

What causes depression? Depression is by no means clearly understood, but as America's most common mood disorder, its origins are many. Most experts say a combination of organic (chemical) or physiological causes underlie depression. Nutrient deficiencies, drugs of all kinds - prescription, recreational, alcohol, caffeine, nicotine, etc., hypoglycemia, sluggish thyroid, hormonal imbalance, allergies and environmental chemicals are just some of the identified factors. Here are some of the surrounding signs that accompany depression:

    1: the inability to mourn or express grief after great loss, such as that of a spouse or child.
    2: bottled-up anger and aggression turned inward.
    3: behavior, often learned as a child, that gets desired attention or controls relationships.
    4: a habitually negative outlook expressed as feelings of pessimism and hopelessness.
    5: biochemical body imbalance characterized by amino acid deficiencies, and monoamines imbalances of serotonin, epinephrine and norepinephrine.
    6: drug-induced depression from prescription drugs, alcohol, caffeine or sugars.
    7: severe, long term stress that weakens and imbalances the nervous system.

Are you depressed? The American Psychiatric Association says you probably are if you have *five* of the following eight symptoms for at least a month.

    1: Poor appetite with weight loss or increased appetite with weight gain.
    2: Insomnia or sleeping excessively (hypersomnia).
    3: Hyperactivity (going a mile a minute) or doing almost nothing all day.
    4: Loss of interest or pleasure in usual activities, usually decrease in sexual drive.
    5: Low energy - great tiredness.
    6: Feelings of worthlessness, self-reproach or inappropriate guilt.
    7: Diminished ability to think or concentrate.
    8: Recurrent thoughts of death or suicide.

You can help yourself if you're depressed. Most health professionals agree that diet improvement and control is one of the critical first steps, because nutrition is essential for brain health. If you are taking MAO inhibitor drugs, control your diet with care. Avoid alcohol, cheese, red meat, yeast extracts and most legumes - foods rich in tyrosine.

Here's my anti-depression diet — a good way to start:

1) Get plenty of healthy protein (about 15% of total calorie intake) to minimize depression. Include protein from seafoods, sea plants, rice, sprouts, soy foods, nuts, seeds, organic turkey and chicken, eggs and low fat cheeses to control depression-related tissue destruction. Amino acids in protein foods help build healthy neurotransmitters for coping with depression. Add foods rich in the amino acid L-tryptophan (soy, cheeses and turkey) to help build serotonin, essential for overcoming depression and insomnia.

2) Have a green salad every day. Sprinkle on 2 TBS. of a mix of lecithin granules, brewer's yeast, wheat germ, pumpkin seeds and use a lemon-canola oil dressing.

3) Have at least 4 other servings of vegetables and some whole grains daily. You'll automatically be eating foods rich in calcium, potassium, iron, magnesium and B vitamins that are usually low in a depressed person's body.

4) Have an adrenal tonic 2 to 3x a week: a glass of carrot juice with a pinch of sage and 1 teasp. Bragg's Liquid Aminos for adrenal stress.

5) Add a superfood daily for "extra strength" nutrition. Some good superfoods to choose from: Crystal Star Systems Strength™, GreenFoods Wheat Germ Extract, Etherium Technology LifeSource, Beehive Botanicals Royal Jelly With Ginseng.

6) Avoid sugary foods, alcohol and caffeine, especially if you have hypoglycemic depression; they wreak havoc on blood sugar levels. Avoid preservative and coloring-laden foods if you have allergy-related depression.

7) Add Omega-3 rich foods to your diet from cold water fish or flax seed. Omega-3 fatty acids are essential to brain health, helping the neurotransmitters norepinephrine and serotonin perform their functions in the brain. A deficiency of Omega-3's is linked to depression.

8) Drink plenty of *bottled* water each day. Dehydration is often linked to depression. Treated water can cause neurotransmitter imbalances.

Can you really use herbs or supplements instead of antidepressant drugs?

Depression is closely linked to low levels of two neurotransmitters in the brain, particularly serotonin, known as the brain's mood-elevater and tranquilizer. Modern psychiatry focuses on manipulating neurotransmitter levels in the brain, so most anti-depressant drugs include monoamine oxidase inhibitors, tricyclic antidepressants, and SSRIs (selective serotonin reuptake inhibitors) which typically work to inhibit the reuptake of serotonin or prevent its breakdown — in essence, increasing the effects of serotonin. Antidepressant drugs can be useful for helping a severely depressed person get "over the hump" during particularly difficult times.

Long term anti-depressants can drain nervous system reservoirs and sap vitality. The chemical side effects of the drugs like weight gain, headaches, sleep disturbances (including insomnia and hypersomnia), fatigue, or tremor, can be unpleasant. I believe, having seen numerous side effects myself, that anti-depressant drugs are best used cautiously, for a limited time, as part of a total program for mental well-being. A program that includes identifying and eliminating psychological factors which cause the neurotransmitter imbalance in the first place, that has a strengthening supportive diet, normalizing tonic herbs, plenty of rest, breathing exercises, and stress reduction tecniques works well. I also believe anti-depressant drug therapy should be monitored closely by your physician so drugs can be changed, reduced or withdrawn safely as needed.

Natural alternatives are often effective for depression because reduced serotonin levels involved in depression are largely caused by dietary and lifestyle factors — like nutrient deficiencies, smoking, alcohol abuse, high sugar intake, or overconsumption of protein. These elements reduce serotonin by impairing the conversion of tryptophan to serotonin. Natural serotonin boosters include St. John's Wort and 5-HTP.

St. John's Wort has been used for over 2,000 years for a wide variety of health needs (an herb is never one plant for one problem). Its benefits range from fighting viruses, to fighting inflammation, to controlling excess weight. Modern alternative medicine focuses on its anti-depression activity almost exclusively. Modern double-blind studies show that *St. John's Wort* produces as good or better results as anti-depressant drugs. Germany uses *St. John's Wort* as its leading treatment, writing more than 3 million prescriptions a year - 25 times the number written for Prozac.

St. John's Wort has virtually no side effects when used correctly, a big plus, since reported side effects for Prozac, like nausea, diarrhea, indigestion, tremor, increased sweating, dry mouth are fairly widespread and unpleasant. The most feared side effect is impaired erections in men, and the inability to achieve orgasm in both men and women. Some people have had to quit Prozac in order to reinstate their libido and ability to have sex.

Transition from Prozac to *St. John's Wort* is best done with a health practitioner — slowly decreasing Prozac dosage—slowly increasing *St. John's Wort.* Crystal Star DEPRESSEX™ (with *St. John's wort, kava kava, gotu kola, panax ginseng, ashwagandha, scullcap, Siberian ginseng, rosemary, wood betony, fo-ti and ginger*) has been effective for many people for years. It provides a measure of calm during grief, anxiety or lingering depression. Results are noticed almost immediately and are reported to be cumulative against depression. I've also used Herbs Etc. DEPREZAC effectively and Allergy Research Group PROZA PLEX.

Kava Kava, a pacific island plant gaining popularity in Europe for treatment of depression compares favorably to benzodiazepine drugs in effectiveness. Kava doesn't carry the side effects of benzodiazepines (impaired mental acuity, addictiveness), either. See Kava Kava, page 18.

Ginkgo Biloba is especially useful for elderly people susceptible to depression or impaired mental function. As people age, a significant reduction in serotonin receptor sites on brain cells occurs. Studies show that ginkgo may counteract some, if not all, of the age-dependent, reduced serotonin binding sites in the brain so serotonin levels remain at more youthful levels. Consider Crystal Star GINKGO BILOBA 100% EXTRACT, or Wakunaga GINKGO-GO or GINKGO BILOBA PLUS.

5-HTP: It's a relatively new answer from the supplement world for mild depression. Take 5-HTP the same day you take a good B-complex 100mg for best uptake results.

5-HTP (L-5-Hydroxytryptophan) is derived from L-Tryptophan, a dietary, essential amino acid that helps synthesize serotonin in our bodies. Tryptophan itself, a powerful supplement in safe use for 25 years prior to 1990, was banned by the FDA when several deaths occurred from a tainted batch by a Japanese company (Showa Denko). Although tryptophan itself was not the cause of the deaths and was cleared of the crime, it has been kept off of the market by the FDA.

Dedicated tryptophan customers who didn't want to resort to drugs demanded a supplement to replace tryptophan, and 5-HTP was born. Many researchers consider 5-HTP derived from the seed of African Griffonia herb, the safest tryptophan alternative available. It is one step closer to serotonin manufacture from trytophan, safer because it is extracted from the seed of a plant instead of synthesized with the help of bacteria. Many studies show 5-HTP helps alleviate serotonin-deficiency symptoms, including depession by naturally elevating brain serotonin.

Here's the 5-HTP background so you can decide for yourself. Serotonin, 5-hydroxytryptamine (5-HT), is a neurotransmitter with widespread, profound actions. When tryptophan is taken up into a nerve cell, it is converted into 5-HTP, then to Serotonin (5-HT), where it plays a role in sleep (it's a precursor to the neurohormone melatonin), mood, appetite, memory, learning, body temperature, sexuality, cardiovascular, nerve and muscle health and gland balance.

If serotonin is low or out of balance in your body, you will probably have increased susceptibility to insomnia, anxiety, depression and migraines. People with low serotonin are likely to be more driven by addictive appetites (food, sex, drugs), and more impulsive (less able to control their behavior). Medical practice treats these types of disorders with SSRIs (selective serotonin reuptake inhibitors) to increase serotonin effects. But side effects are an unpleasant problem with SSRIs (Prozac). 5-HTP offers many of the benefits of a SSRI with few if any side effects. Still, 5-HTP shouldn't be taken with antidepressant drugs, MAO inhibitors, SSRIs (Prozac), tricyclic medication, prescription weight loss drugs, anti-Parkinson medication (L-dopa), barbiturates or other tranquilizers, (5-HTP potentiates their effects), alcoholic beverages, chemotherapy, antihistamines or antibiotic drugs.

50 to 100 mg a day is a common dose for 5-HTP. Vitamin B-6 (pyridoxine) is required for the enzymatic conversion of 5-HTP into serotonin. Allergy Research 5-HTP (L-5-Hydroxytryptophan) and Natural Balance HTP. CALM were effective for the Healthy Healing test group.

Note 1: **Rhodiola,** a Russian herb just appearing in this country, has been proven, after 35 years of successful research in the Russian military, to enhance the transport of tryptophan and 5-HTP into the brain, exerting inhibitory effects on MAO (monoamine oxidase) and COMT (catechol-o-methyltransferase) neurotransmitter activity, for a 30% boost in brain serotonin levels. Natural Balance RHODIOLA is the brand we tested.

Note 2: **S-Adenosyl-Methionine (SAM):** New clinical studies show that SAM (impaired in depressed patients) is an effective natural anti-depressant. SAM is normally produced in the brain from the amino acid methionine. Supplementing with SAM results in increased levels of serotonin and dopamine in the brain with improved binding of neurotransmitters to receptor sites. SAM has a quicker onset of action and is better tolerated than tricyclic anti-depressants.

Are you anxious? Do you feel like a "bundle of nerves?" What if you're not really depressed, just full of worry?

Mild anxiety, unease, periodic nervousness, even fear are part of life. They're normal stress reactions that pass as life goes on. But stress has gotten to such a state in America today that more than 14 million Americans carry anxiety with them all the time instead of letting it pass.

Here are some of the signs:

—Have you lost interest in things you used to find enjoyable?

—Do the corners of your eyes sag? Do you look noticeably older? Is your brow furrowed?

—Have you become short-tempered or easily angered? easily bored or nervous?

—Are you tired or sad all the time? Do you have frequent insomnia?

—Do you have chronic head and neck aches? a chronic upset stomach?

—Is your blood pressure high? Do you get heart palpitations?

—Are you susceptible to frequent allergic reactions, especially skin disorders?

—Does your chest feel tight? Do you have trouble taking in enough air?

Anxiety and extreme nervousness are symptoms of severe stress. Chronic, severe stress imbalances body chemistry, creating an over acid system - specifically a higher ratio of lactic acid to pyruvic acid than normal. Rebalancing lactate (the soluble form of lactic acid) levels in the body should be part of an anxiety reducing program.

—Reduce alcohol, tobacco, caffeine and sugar. They elevate lactic acid.

Alcohol, a brain depressant, interferes with many brain cell processes, it increases adrenal hormone output and disrupts normal sleep cycles. Alcohol causes blood sugar to drop, resulting in sugar cravings, often leading to hypoglycemia. Hypoglycemia aggravates mental and emotional problems (symptoms include anxiety, irritability and fatigue). Eliminating alcohol and sugar is a major step for people whose anxiety or paranoia results from reactive hypoglycemia.

Caffeine, in heavy use can produce symptoms like nervousness, heart palpitations, irritability, headaches, even paranoia. For some people simply eliminating coffee can result in complete symptom relief. Combining caffeine and sugar compounds the negative effects.

Smoking (nicotine) stimulates adrenal secretion, including cortisol, linked to anxiety and panic attacks. Smoking contributes to vitamin C deficiency; low levels of vitamin C in the brain are regularly involved in nervous, depressive states.

—Add B vitamins to your diet, with plenty of leafy greens, brown rice and sea foods; or take a B-complex vitamin 100mg daily. Add 5000mg of vitamin C daily for at least 1 month.

—Add minerals to your diet, with plenty of leafy greens and whole grains; or take a full-spectrum mineral supplement, like TRACE-LYTE from Nature's Path.

—Lack of essential omega-3 fatty acids may contribute to panic attacks and anxiety reactions. Add flaxseed oil 1 TB. daily to your diet, or take *evening primrose oil* 1000mg daily.

Beyond foods, many herbs are rich in calcium and magnesium, Nature's primary mineral elements for calming and stabilizing nerves. Crystal Star CALCIUM SOURCE™ (with *watercress, oatstraw, rosemary, dandelion, alfalfa, pau d' arco, borage and carrot)* is also rich in organic silica for bone, tissue and collagen strength.

Crystal Star STRESSED OUT™ EXTRACT (with *black cohosh, scullcap, black haw, wood betony, kava kava and carrot extract)* is one of the most effective fomulas available for relieving nerve and muscle pain. It is strong enough to deal with severe symptoms, yet soothing and restorative. It helps the adrenals respond to stress by increasing utilization of ascorbic acid stores. It aids repair of nerve sheathing and uses rich herbal minerals to control acid-produced stress.

Crystal Star STRESSED-OUT™ TEA (with *chamomile, rosemary, peppermint, catnip feverfew, heartsease, white willow, wood betony and blessed thistle)* is particularly effective for tension head, neck and shoulder aches. It may also be used to calm hyperactive children.

Most highly anxious people constantly worry, so they have trouble getting enough sleep — the very thing that can most quickly improve the body's ability to deal with their stress. New studies show that over 15% of the American population (36 million people), take sedative drugs for insomnia stress symptoms. Most of these prescriptions are highly addictive benzodiazepine compounds, like Valium (30 million prescriptions). The studies also show that almost 50 million additional people regularly use over-the-counter sleeping pills. While the abusive/addictive potential of these medications is not as great, the body builds a certain immunity to them. More and more drug needs to be taken to get the same effect.

I believe herbal compounds that relax and help rebuild the nervous system are a better choice for many people. Certainly they don't have the serious side effects or potential for addiction. Herbs can be as effective as prescription tranquilizer drugs in overcoming stress insomnia.

Nervine herbs are specifics for nervous system stress. Nervine herbs are nerve restoratives, especially for protective nerve sheathing. Some nervines, like lemon balm, lavender, scullcap and black haw are mild tranquilizers so they address symptoms like insomnia, anxiety and pain. Others like kava kava, gotu kola, rosemary or yerba maté help reassert nerve vitality. The different types of nervine herbs act  through different body pathways; it is far more effective to use them in combination than to take them alone.

Crystal Star RELAX CAPS™ (with *ashwagandha, black cohosh, scullcap, kava kava, black haw, hops, valerian, European mistletoe, wood betony, lobelia and oatstraw)* has been effective for over twenty years as an herbal nervine. It works especially for women's nervousness.

Crysal Star NIGHT CAPS™ (with *valerian, scullcap, passionflower, kava kava, hops and carrot extract)* is especially effective for men, who report that it helps them remember their dreams and encourages deeper REM sleep.

How about the mind's role in anxiety and depression? Does our mental outlook affect our body's stress reactions?

Our daily habits can cause anxiety, too. Habitually negative thought and feeling patterns aren't a normal human trait, but they are a chronic stress reaction. Your thoughts register through your endocrine system, triggering the hypothalmic-pituitary-adrenal axis. Messages from the brain through the nervous system are instantaneous.

Attachment to negative feelings causes nervous system imbalances that affect your brain, heart, hormonal and immune systems. A Harvard Public Health study shows that men with the highest anger scores on personality tests are three times more likely to develop heart disease! A ten year study from the University of Pittsburgh finds that women who bottle up their anger or are easily irritated have more arterial plaque buildup, even thickening of their arteries!

Your mind and body are in constant communication with each other in profound ways. Nutritional deficiencies contribute to emotional and mental stress. Dwelling on negative thoughts like fear, anger or frustration not only affects your mood and personality; it clearly affects your physical health — a powerful message for taking control of your emotional and mental habits.

Your mind is also your greatest personal healer. You can set your mind to work to solve your health problems just as you would any other problem. Your mind can be your most courageous ally against fear, depression and defeat.

Your thoughts are so powerful that they create your life.

Every single experience you have can move you onward and upward, or cast you into unhappiness and depression. It's all in your point of view. We may not have control over stressful things; we do have control over our reactions to them.

The *Journal of Health and Social Behavior* recently studied 200 male executives undergoing grave corporate changes which caused huge stress in their jobs. The researchers discovered that half the men were able to escape stress, while the other half had a host of stress-induced illnesses. The men who looked at the stressful events negatively were devastated. The men who handled the stress well looked at the problems as a stepping-stone to the desired goal.

Of course you have to deal with problems. Just look for the good things in your life while you're handling the problems, instead of focusing on the future or an impending problem. Concentrate on using a "bad" event or a failure as a mechanism through which you learn to do things right. At times, this may be extremely difficult, but as long as you are alive, nothing is a foregone conclusion. Everything changes and passes. You can determine the outcome of your world and your life almost entirely from your thoughts.

You can learn the skills of taking negative thinking and transforming it into positive thinking. You can escape negative mind chatter and steer your mind back onto a positive road.

• You can learn to recognize the automatic negative thoughts that move through your consciousness when you feel depressed.

• Since every human experience has both a positive and negative aspect, you can change negative thinking by re-examining the problem for its positive side.

• You can gain control of your thoughts by seeing how they constantly churn in your mind and replacing them with empowering positive thoughts and beliefs.

Our thoughts and emotions have an impact on our body's internal pharmacy.

Clearly mental, emotional and spiritual well-being shapes physical health. A program of stress management and rejuvenation is incomplete unless we manage our thoughts and emotions so that they serve us instead of harming us. Countless studies show that mental stress in particular, has a serious impact on heart problems like high blood pressure, asthma, gastritis, obesity, insomnia, premature aging, and a compromised immune system.

Can you really manage your thoughts and feelings? Can we "detox" our minds?

All of us are trying to pay attention to our diets and avoid environmental toxins, but few of us understand the importance of our mental and emotional diets. Long term negative thoughts and emotions can be as damaging as toxic chemicals. The way we function mentally and emotionally is a major contributor to self nurturing or self poisoning.

When your body is under stress, the nervous system responds by increasing *sympathetic* activity. In other words, it creates nervous restlessness, hyperactivity, anxiety, muscle tension, cardiovascular stress, etc. Stress creates specific hormonal imbalances that can damage brain cells, too. If the stress is prolonged, the adrenal and pituitary glands produce degenerative stress-fighting hormones, to provide emergency relief... at a price. (Chemical waste is produced, which degenerates nerve cells and causes free radical damage.)

Studies show that feelings of happiness and joy increase white blood cell counts needed for healing and defending against invading organisms.

Here are some new techniques from The Institute of HeartMath™ **you can personally access to help manage your thoughts and emotions.** IHM is a nonprofit research organization specializing in reducing stress and dramatically improving the body's physiology. IHM has pioneered bio-medical research showing the relationship between feelings, the heart, mental/emotional balance, cardiovascular function, hormones and immune system health.

HeartMath bases its work on the theory that mental and emotional response causes electrical changes in the heart, nervous system and brain. The electrical changes directly affect your heart rate, blood pressure, hormonal and immune responses which in turn influence your state of well-being and whether you become stressed or not.

Because the heart generates the most powerful electromagnetic field in the body, every cell receives the heart's message. Heart rate variability (the beat-to-beat changes in heart rate as the heart speeds up and slows down) analysis has proven an invaluable monitoring tool into the nature of the healing process. Along with looking at HRV patterns, scientists also analyze *electrocardiograms* to see the effects of hostility and depression. Only recently, through the use of ECG spectral analysis, have more subtle "negative" emotions, like frustration, worry, and anxiety, and "positive" emotions such as love, care, compassion, and appreciation been visible.

If you are having a day where life seems to be falling apart, your ECG graphs have a jagged appearance, an "incoherent spectrum." If you are having a day where you're feeling on top of the world, your ECG graphs have a harmonious, "coherent spectrum." Feelings such as love, care or compassion create even more "cohesion" power in the graphs.

Two amazing HeartMath studies:

HeartMath' techniques called FREEZE-FRAME™ exercise and CUT-THRU™ exercise can effectively dissolve repeated negative thought patterns. You can:
- Reduce burnout from overload, stress, anxiety and indecision.
- Boost anti-aging hormones and your immune system.
- Access free energy and increase your personal effectiveness.
- Achieve what you usually can't because of the effects of negative thought habits.

Some reports seem almost miraculous using the HeartMath tests. Patients with a variety of disorders report significant improvements in their symptomatology after practicing the HeartMath interventions even for short periods of time.

The Freeze-Frame exercise: An exercise called *"Freeze-Frame,"* actually produces chemical and electrical changes in the body. When a patient is asked to recall or imagine being loved, for example, the heart responds by literally vibrating at a different energy frequency. The response is instantaneously picked up by the brain, which sends messages via neurotransmitter pathways telling the body's endocrine system to generate hormones in doses that foster health. The result is an almost immediate heightened state of well-being marked by greater energy, and greater tolerance for things that would normally be frustrating and stressful. One test patient reported "I watched the pattern of my angry heartbeats rise and fall across a computer screen in jagged spikes. When I began *Freeze-Frame* and imagined being loved, my heartbeat rhythm settled into a smoother, even pattern, like ripples in a pond, and continued that way as long as I practiced *Freeze-Frame."*

The Cut-Thru Technique: This technique powerfully documents the effects of stress busting exercises by tracking levels of the hormones DHEA and cortisol. Low DHEA levels have been linked to fatigue, exhaustion, muscle weakness, immune disorders, PMS, obesity, diabetes and Alzheimer's disease. Increased DHEA levels reduce depression, anxiety, memory loss and premature anti-aging. In Cut-Thru studies, levels of DHEA rose from 100 percent to triple or quadruple their pre-Cut-Thru levels after test subjects practiced the technique for one month. The subjects did not change their diets or make any other life-style changes.

Emotional stressors like guilt, anxiety, or anger can cause high levels of the stress hormone cortisol which damage brain cells and accelerate aging. After practicing the Cut-Thru technique for a month, cortisol levels in test subjects dropped an average of 23 percent.

The Institute of HeartMath is an innovative nonprofit research organizantion which has developed simple, user-friendly tools to relieve stress and to break through into greater levels of personal balance and creativity. Contact them at: Institute of HeartMath, P.O. Box 1463, 14700 West Park Ave., Boulder Creek, CA 95006, 800-450-9111, www.heartmath.org.

More mind-body connection techniques:

How does guided imagery work for stress and depression? Stress reduction techniques, like meditation and guided imagery, powerfully affect both the onset and progression of disease. Studies show both meditation and imagery help people eliminate or reduce the severity and frequency of headaches, slow down the aging process dramatically, manage the discomfort of lower back pain, heart disease, hypertension, irritable bowel syndrome, even cancer and AIDS.

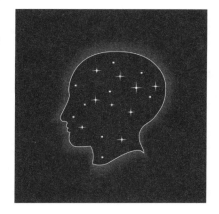

Imagery is simply a flow of thoughts that you can see, hear, feel, smell, or taste in your imagination. It's the way your nervous system processes information, so it's especially effective for the dialogue between mind and body in the healing process.

Imagery assists "in clarifying attitudes, emotions, behavior and lifestyle patterns that may be involved in illness." Guided imagery is a proven method for pain relief, for helping people tolerate medical procedures, for reducing side effects, and for stimulating healing response. It can help people find meaning in their illness, offer a way to cope, and accelerate recovery.

Learning to relax is fundamental to self-healing, and imagery is a part of almost all relaxation and stress-reduction techniques. For many people, imagery is an easy way to learn to relax, and its active nature makes it more comfortable than other methods.

Stress is an excellent example of an emotional response that manifests itself in the body.
Here's an example: a man might respond to the loss of his wife with a prolonged state of depression. His body too, will be in a state of depression, making him susceptible to serious health problems. But if he is able to intergrate his loss into a broader meaning of life by directly accessing emotions through guided imagery, his loss won't totally overwhelm him, and his grief will lessen over time. Gradually, he can develop a more wholesome view of his life, to again become a participant, rather than a victim of its circumstances.

There are two types of guided imagery:
• Receptive imagery guides you into a relaxed state, then concentrates your focus on the area of your body that is ailing, to envision an embodiment of the illness (like a mischievous imp) and ask it why it is causing the trouble.
• Active imagery envisions the illness being cured. This may mean anything from imagining your immune system attacking a tumor to picturing pain as a ball rolling out of your body.

I believe in massage therapy for stress relief. The worst result of stress is fatigue. Massage therapy deals directly with skeletal-muscular areas where fatigue shows up - the stiff neck, the tight shoulders, the aching back. During massage, constricted muscles get stretched and relaxed to improve circulation, which increases energy and reduces anxiety.

Massage therapists learn a nurturing touch — long, flowing strokes that can alleviate even severe depression. More massage is better in my opinion — once a week is good, twice a week is excellent if you suffer from chronic anxiety. Regularity is important, since a tell-tale attribute of serious depression is that the feeling of well-being can't last. The actual anti-depressant effects of a half hour massage last from 3 to 36 hours. More importantly, it re-educates your body. A regular therapeutic massage helps your body "remember" what it feels like to be comfortable, relaxed and cared for. I, myself, have experienced this phenomenon.

Here's what I notice during a massage therapy treatment. As your body stops feeling stressed, it relaxes, and goes into a restorative mode. You can feel it. Your breathing slows down, as extra oxygen needs decline. Your heart slows down its pump rate, allowing tense arterial muscles to relax and blood pressure to decrease. As anxiety wanes, serum lactate and cortisol levels reduce, so you stop extra sweating and salivating. At your body's deepest levels, your sympathetic nervous system, designed to protect you against danger, reverts to its normal "stand-by" mode, and your parasympathetic nervous system, designed to keep your body repaired and maintained, becomes dominant once again.

Special Stress Busters

Beyond diet, supplement and herbs, there are other highly effective stress busters that can return your energy and well-being. They could be just what you need.

Aromatherapy & Stress

Healers have known for thousands of years that volatile aromas of essential oils directly affect the brain, some producing calming effects, others mental stimulation. Today, aromatherapy is experiencing a renaissance. Therapists of all kinds are once again using essential oils for their healing art. They are some of the most potent of all herbal medicines.

Essential oils, 75 to 100 times more concentrated than dried herbs and flowers, are the heart of aromatherapy. They are volatile liquids that act in plants much like hormones do in humans. They are the regenerating and oxygenating immune defense properties of plants.

Essential oils carry a bio-electrical frequency - a measurable rate of electrical energy that is constant between any two points. Everything has an electrical frequency, measured in hertz:
—Food has a frequency from 0 to15Hz.
—Dry herbs are from15 to 22Hz.
—Fresh herbs are 20 to 27Hz.
—Essential aromatherapy oils start at 52Hz and go to 320Hz (rose oil is 320Hz).
—A healthy body usually has a frequency between 62 to 78Hz.
—Disease begins at 58Hz. A higher frequency destroys a disease of lower frequency.

Essential oils have a physical impact on the body: Essential oils create an environment in which disease, bacteria, virus, and fungus cannot live. The majority of essential oils affect microorganisms that are resistant to antibiotics. They have antibacterial, antiviral, antifungal, anti-inflammatory and anti-parasitic activity.

Essential oils are best known for counteracting stress, with properties which can affect the mind and emotions to calm, sedate or uplift.

The immediate and profound effect of essential oils on the central nervous system makes aromatherapy an excellent method for stress management. Aromatherapy also makes us feel good in part by releasing certain mood-inducing neurochemicals in our brains. Aromatherapy relieves stress by promoting mental relaxation and alertness, quality sleep, physical relaxation, and by increasing overall energy.

How does Aromatherapy work?

Aromatherapy's oils effect different people in different ways, on different levels. Aroma itself is only one of the active healing qualities. The oils exert much of their therapeutic effect through pharmacological properties and their small molecular size. They are one of the few medicinal agents easily absorbed by the body. The oxygenating molecules of essential oils transport nutrients directly to our cells.

How many times have you smelled something like a perfume or a food and had the taste of it instantly in your mouth? The volatile molecules of the perfume or food enter your nose and can be tasted in your mouth.

Essential oils affect people first through the sense of smell. Smell is the most rapid of all the senses because its information is directly relayed to the hypothalamus. Motivation, moods and creativity all begin in the hypothalamus, so odors affect all of these processes. Scents are intimately intertwined with our emotions, feelings, and memories. Certain oils can enhance your emotional equilibrium merely by inhaling them. When inhaled, the odors stimulate a release of neurotransmitters, chemicals responsible for pleasant feelings and pain reduction.

Scents also influence the endocrine system responsible for hormone levels, metabolism, insulin production, stress levels, sex drive, body temperature and appetite. The volatile molecules of essential oils work through hormone-like chemicals. Studies done on brain-waves show that scents (like lavender) increase alpha brain waves associated with relaxation; scents (like jasmine) boost beta waves linked with alertness. The aromas of apples and cinnamon have a powerful stabilizing effect on some people, especially those suffering from nervous anxiety. These aromas are even capable of lowering blood pressure and preventing panic attacks.

Essential oil fluids are volatile, non-oily essences. They are highly active, and may be taken in by inhalation, steams and infusers, or applied topically to the skin. The therapeutic effects of essential oils are due both to their pharmacological properties and their small molecular size, which allows penetration through the skin, the walls of the blood vessels, the lymph system and body tissues. These pathways allow essential oils to strengthen and tone the body's organ, hormonal, nervous and immune systems. Essential oils applied to the skin can reach muscle tissue and joints, the bloodstream, body tissues and organs.

Here's how to use aromatherapy: Add a few drops of essential oil into a carrier oil such as almond, jojoba or a favorite massage oil. Use a diffuser or lamp, or a steam inhaler to ease respiratory distress. When inhaled into the lungs, molecules of essential oils attach to oxygen molecules, enter the bloodstream and journey throughout the body with therapeutic activity. Oils evaporate easily and completely. They don't leave marks on your clothing or towels.

- Always dilute essential oils in a carrier oil, such as almond, apricot, canola or jojoba oil, before applying them. Essential oils are highly concentrated. Even one drop of pure essential oil applied directly to your skin may cause irritation.
- Uncap oil bottles for a few seconds only or they'll escape. Drop oils into the palm of your hand for blending. Keep bottles tightly capped, away from sunlight and heat when not in use.
- Follow the directions for aromatherapy blends carefully. Never add more than the recommended number of drops. When using essential oils on infants or children, dilute them.
- Use glass containers for all blends of essential oils. Oils can damage plastic containers.
- Don't shake essential oils. Just gently roll the bottle between your hands.
- Inhale essential oils for short periods only; run a diffuser for only 5 to 10 minutes at a time.
- If you experience any irritation, sensitivity, or reaction, discontinue use of the suspect oil.
- Don't take essential oils internally, except as directed by a professional.

As always, people with certain medical conditions should be cautious. Some essential oils can trigger asthma attacks or epileptic seizures in susceptible people. Some can elevate or depress blood pressure. Consult a health care professional if you have any of these conditions. Essential oils may diminish the effectiveness of homeopathic remedies. Check with a homeopathic physician.

Reducing stress is an aromatherapy specialty.

I've listed some of the essential aromatherapy oils you can use for stress relief and for energizing. Essential oils have a normalizing effect on the nervous system. For example, *bergamot* (geranium oil) either stimulates or sedates according to the needs of the individual.

Calming, relaxing essential oils to reduce stress:

Lavender: induces sleep, exerts a calming and relaxing effect, alleviates stress, reduces depression, tension and hyperactivity. Can also be used to calm animals. Balances nerves and emotions. Pain relief for headaches. Calms the heart and lowers high blood pressure. Rub on stomach for painful menstrual periods. A tonic for the hair.

Marjoram: calms anxiety. A warming analgesic for pain, stiff joints, colds, asthma, painful periods. A tonic for the heart, lowers high blood pressure. Promotes blood flow in skin. *Note: Take a break after one month of usage.*

Sandalwood: relaxes, good for meditation and sleep. Stimulates immune response. Massage oil over the kidney area for cystitis and kidney problems. Healing and moisturizing for cracked and dry skin; relieves itching and inflammation. An aphrodisiac.

Clary sage: calms edgy nerves, brings feelings of well-being, lifts the mind and reduces stress. A hormone balancer, helpful for PMS cramps and muscle spasms. Useful for all types of skin inflammations and for aging skin and wrinkles.

Geranium: acts as an antidepressant and tonic to the nervous system to reduce tension and stress. Helpful in overcoming addictions. Helps the pituitary gland to regulate the endocrine system and hormone balance. Helps menopause, PMS and through its astringent action, stems heavy periods. Helpful for circulation to the skin, eczema, burns and shingles. Precautions: avoid during pregnancy. A good skin cleanser, but test first for skin sensitivity.

Essential oils for Depression:
Bergamot: an uplifting anti-depressant; relaxes nervous system; good for anxiety. Eases digestion. Helps with eczema, psoriasis and acne. An antiseptic for wounds and urinary tract infections. Precautions: may cause photosensitivity. Avoid hot sun right after use on skin.

Neroli: relieves stress, depression, anxiety, nervous tension and insomnia. Helps headaches. A heart tonic, improves circulation and helps nerve pain. Useful for dry, sensitive skin.

Jasmine: uplifting, soothing, very good for depression; a hormone balancer, known for its erogenous quality. Helpful for menstrual pain and uterine disorders. Helpful for respiratory difficulties, bronchial spasms, catarrh, cough and hoarseness. Especially dry and sensitive skin.

Ylang Ylang: uplifts the mood, eases anxiety, diminishes depression, eases feelings of anger, shock, panic and fear. Balances women's hormones. Helps high blood pressure and insomnia. Balances sebum flow to stimulate scalp for hair growth.

Essential oils for energizing and motivating:
Lavender: (see previous page).

Cypress: calms irritability, and stress reactions like sweating. Balances body fluids, and helps release cellulite. Helps nose bleeds, heavy periods, incontinence. Soothes sore throats. An astringent for oily skin, hemorrhoids and varicose veins. Precautions: avoid in pregnancy.

Ginger: sharpens senses and aids memory. Helps settle the digestive system, colds, flu and reduces fever. Helps motion sickness, nausea, gas and pain. Add to massage rubs for rheumatic pains and bone injuries, sores and bruises. Precautions: may irritate skin.

Rosemary: encourages intuition, enlivens the brain, clears the head (helps headaches) and enhances memory. For exhaustion, weakness and lethargy. A sinus decongestant. Pain relieving properties for arthritis, gout, and sore muscles. A heart tonic, normalizes low blood pressure. Precautions: avoid during pregnancy, with high blood pressure or epilepsy.

Note: The essential oils and blends in this section can be obtained from your health food store or Wyndmere Naturals 153 Ashley Road, Hopkins, MN 55343, 800-207-8538.

Stress reduction and relaxation recipes:

•**Stress-Soothing Massage Oil:** to 2 ounces sweet almond oil, add 4 drops bergamot oil, 4 drops chamomile oil, 4 drops lavender oil, 4 drops sandalwood oil, 3 drops marjoram oil, 2 drops elemi oil and 2 drops frankincense oil.

•**Stress-Buster Diffuser Oil:** combine 15 drops lavender oil, 10 drops sage oil, 10 drops elemi oil, 10 drops geranium oil, 8 drops bergamot oil, 8 drops orange oil, 8 drops rosewood oil, 6 drops ylang ylang oil and 5 drops coriander oil. Add a few drops to your diffuser or lamp bowl.

Energy stimulation - Some essential oils have a direct effect on the central nervous system. Peppermint energizes while easing headaches. Ginger and fennel stimulate circulation, all the way from your heart to your fingertips. Rose influences hormonal activity and glandular function. Lavender and geranium can either stimulate or sedate, according to the individual's physiological needs.

•**Energizing Body Oil:** mix, then massage into skin in the morning, 2 ounces sweet almond oil, 6 drops lavender oil, 4 drops rosemary oil, 3 drops geranium oil, 3 drops lemon oil, 2 drops coriander oil, 2 drops patchouli oil.

•**Energy Inhalant Oil:** in a small glass bottle, combine 8 drops rosemary oil, 6 drops elemi oil, 4 drops peppermint oil, 3 drops basil oil, 1 drop ginger oil. Inhale directly from the bottle for an energy boost.

•**Energy Boosting Diffuser Blend Oil:** in a small glass bottle, combine 15 drops rosemary oil, 12 drops pine oil, 10 drops lavender oil, 10 drops lemon oil, 2 drops peppermint oil. Add a few drops to your diffuser or lamp bowl.

•**Fatigue-Fighting Bath Oil:** to your bath, add 4 drops rosemary oil, 2 drops orange oil, 1 drop thyme oil.

Flower essence therapy and stress

Flower essences are part of an emerging field of life-enhancing subtle therapies, that work through human energy fields to address issues of emotional health and mind-body well-being. Like homeopathy and acupuncture, they are exceptions to western type science. Like homeopathic remedies, flower essences, although highly dilute from a physical point of view, are *potentized vibrational tinctures* from the patterns of biomagnetic energies discharged by flowers. Flowers are the highest concentration of the life force in the plant, the crowning experience of the plants' growth. Flower essences are captured at the highest moment of the plant unfolding in blossom. The essence is generally prepared from a sun infusion of blossoms in a bowl of water, which is potentized, then preserved with brandy.

The healing art of flower essences is used today by almost every healing discipline — medical and health practitioners, homeopaths, massage therapists, chiropractors, psychotherapists, counsellors, dentists and veterinarians.

The application of flower essences for specific emotions and attitudes was developed by Dr. Edward Bach, an English physician and homeopath in the 1930s. Bach's research showed that flowers discharge identified patterns of biomagnetic energies that could be harnessed for healing power through emotional balance. Bach's work on the relationship of stress to disease showed that the link between the mind and body is most evident during stressful situations. He also showed the significance of destructive emotions like depression, hate and fear.

Bach was one of the first modern healers to realize that true healing means the materialization of one's higher spiritual force. He saw that emotional balance strengthened the body's ability to resist disease. In the last decade, modern medicine is also beginning to see the connection between negative emotions and lower disease resistance. Deepak Chopra M.D., a well-known expert in the new field of psycho-neuro-immunology (mind-body connection), says that, "The mind is in every cell of the body. Every thought we think releases neuropeptides that are transmitted to all the cells."

Emotional stress disrupts nerve functions, hormone levels and immune response. Loving thoughts release interleukin and interferon, body healers. Anxious thoughts release cortisone and adrenaline which suppress the immune system. Peaceful thoughts release body chemicals similar to valium, which relax.

Flower essences can be a healing tool to assist us in emotional, mental and spiritual balance. Flower essence case studies show that people taking the remedies often experience physical and spiritual cleansing as well as emotional purification.

Bach was able to document scientifically the clinical criteria that is still used today in flower essence research. His compound, Rescue Remedy, is the most widely used flower essence — a gentle, effective remedy which restores the system's emotional balance during stress or anxiety. It can also be used in emergency situations or at any time of upset, shock or trauma, like impending events which produce anxiety (before giving a speech, or going to the dentist) or for working in an atmosphere of unrelenting stress.

"What Bach was doing with his vibrational essences was working to increase his patients' resistance by creating internal harmony and an amplification of the higher energetic systems that connect human beings to their higher selves." Richard Gerber, M.D. *Vibrational Medicine*.

Flower Essences that can assist stress reduction:

Deva Flower Remedies has formulated *combination blends* of selected flower essences that treat generalized mental and emotional disorders.

I recommend the following:

• STRESS/TENSION - Clears mental strain and pressure, relaxes tense muscles and calms and strengthens the nervous system. Eases headaches and other pain.

• ANXIETY - For nervous, restless, distressed, or unsettled feelings.

• DEPRESSION/GLOOM - Feeling the blues, down, disheartened, trapped, discouraged or having great sorrow. Over-shadowed by dark cloud or having a disassociated mental state.

• FEARFULNESS - Fearful feelings such as fear of darkness, being attacked, aging and dying, being alone, illnes, loss of control, etc. Dreading life or feeling panicky and terrified.

- **WORRY/CONCERN** - Worry about aging and death. Hidden worries over misfortune befalling yourself or a loved one.
- **FATIGUE/EXHAUSTION** - Tired, burned out, burdened by life, excessive performance pressure, lack of vitality and strength, or a physical or mental breakdown.

Note: The remedies on this and the previous page are available at your health food store or from DEVA FLOWER REMEDIES @ Natural Labs, P.O. Box 20037, Sedona, AZ 86341, 800-233-0810.

BACH FLOWER REMEDIES produces the well known product, RESCUE REMEDY, (see previous page) for stress and emergency situations that cause emotional stress. RESCUE REMEDY contains essences of *cherry plum*, for fear of losing control, *clematis*, for resignation and fatalism, *impatiens*, for anxiousness, *rock rose*, for panic and terror, and *star of Bethlehem*, for shock and fright.

Nelson Bach, Wilmington Technology Park, 100 Research Drive, Wilmington MA 01887-4406, 800-319-9151.

Polarity therapy.... a new technique to reduce stress?

Many respected researchers believe today that aberrated electromagnetic fields or wavelengths (such as EMFs) introduce an antagonistic response to man's otherwise harmonious energies frequencies. Robert Becker, M.D. author of *The Body Electric* says, "We now live in a sea of electromagnetic radiation that we cannot sense and that never before existed on this earth. New evidence suggests that this massive amount of radiation is producing stress, disease and other harmful effects by interfering with the most basic levels of brain function."

Our society is so dependent on electronics that abolishing electromagnetic radiation is out of the question. But we may be able to protect the body's life force energies with things like Polarity devices which act as "antennas" or "waveguides" to attract and reinforce healthful wave-lengths to the body. Beneficial wave-lengths have been known since the 1950's (first identified by Bell Science Labs).

Subtle biological healing energies appear to be composed of a combination of subtle energy fields — electromagnetic fields; and underlying quantum fields. Quantum fields propagate without loss of energy (unlike traditional electromagnetic waves). They also have a unique ability to focus their energy (converge rather than diverge) which helps explain how subtle energy devices can focus their energy to create subtle energy healing effects. The combination of the fields appears to boost stress-reducing biochemical mediators. In fact, researchers say healing can never be explained without paying attention to the underlying energetic fields that may be primary to initiating the healing response.

Polarizers reset vortex spins so that they are consistent with positive life force. North of the Earth's equator, a toxic vortex spins counter-clockwise and a healthy vortex spins clockwise. (South of the equator the reverse is true.) Polarizers work to repolarize or respin the negative vortex action, to either neutralize it or carry it into a beneficial spin.

There is clinical evidence today for the effectiveness of this blend of quantum physics applied to biology and medicine. When polarity devices are brought in close contact to areas of pain or muscle tension many people reported pain relief and a greater sense of well-being. In geriatrics treatment and home health nursing, numerous case studies show that polarizers make significant health improvement in many patients. Relaxation, reduced fatigue, reduced mental confusion, improved sleep, pain relief, and improvement of allergy symptoms are just a few of the benefits.

If you're interested.... SPRINGLIFE POLARIZERS, Springlife Inc., 4630 N. Paseo Delos Cerritos, Tucson, AZ 85745, 888-633-9233.

Exercise: unleash the power of movement to release stress.

Exercise may work better than drug tranquilizers for relaxing tension. Just thirty minutes of exercise eases nerves and increases feelings of self-confidence. Regular exercise can reduce muscle tension up to 25 percent, and can reduce anxiety for up to two hours after an exercise session. Depressive symptoms are less likely to continue when an exercise program is established.

Exercise promotes feelings of well-being from morphine-like endorphins.
Exercise significantly reduces anxiety and depression.
Exercise improves sleep.
Exercise gives your blood a tune-up, making red blood cells more elastic.
Exercise promotes focused concentration and better academic
    performance from increased oxygen to the brain.
Exercise boosts circulation, and increases total blood volume because
    your body produces more plasma.
Exercise aids blood viscosity, allowing it to flow more easily, reducing
    the risk of clot formation in the heart and brain.
Exercise focuses your attention inward without distractions. You can
    reflect on your personal world and how it's going. Need to make any changes?

Your exercise doesn't have to be complicated or rigorous. Just get moving. A short 10 to 15 walk minute,something most of us can spare, is a great way to slow down and relieve stress. Besides the physical benefits like improved circulation and oxygen, just the time taken to exercise provides an opportunity to separate ourselves from the demands of our everyday lives.

A small amount of exercise every day brings on a "RELAXATION RESPONSE," a term coined by Herbert Benson, M.D., founder of Mind/Body Medical Institute. According to Dr. Benson, "By repeating a muscular actvity or saying a word, phrase or prayer over and over- for 10 to 20 minutes a day, twice a day, you can reduce the symptoms of stress, increase your sense of well-being and create a feeling of being in control."

A study at Purdue University studied a group of middle-aged professors in a five month walk-jog program who attained significant stress relieving benefits. Their blood chemistry showed a marked reduction of catecholamines (hormones associated with aggression, anxiety and depression), and the professors noticed that they felt more open and extroverted, and self confident.

Stretching, toning exercises done when you rise and before you go to bed are some of my personal favorites. Since stress lodges often in the head, neck and shoulders, stretching exercises can be an effective way to reduce stress and increase flexibility (see Stress and Arthritis, page 65).

Here's an easy set of stretches I've been doing for years:
—Swing both arms like windmills — 10 times forward and ten times backward.
—Bend down and touch the palms of your hands to the floor (or as far as you can reach).
—Do head rolls — all the way around — 5 times to the left, 5 times to the right.
—Stand on your tip toes and reach as high as you can. Take three deep breaths.
—Hands on hips, bend as far as you can to each side back and forth 5 times.

Yoga exercises develop strength, stamina, focus, balance and flexibility. Yoga also emphasizes slow, deep breathing to release stress and create a peaceful mindset. The slower-motion movements of stretching and yoga stimulate the energy-conserving parasympathetic nervous system, which lowers your heart rate and blood pressure and leaves you calm and connected.

Daily stress-busting stretches:
If you have a job that has you sitting at a desk all day, you are likely to suffer a 40% decrease in functional neck strength. Neck stretches ease neck and back pain and they combat stress.

1: Relax your neck: Put one arm up and over your head — grasp your neck below the ear on the opposite side from your arm. Pull your head gently toward your shoulder, and hold. Repeat on the other side.

2: Chin tuck: Sitting or standing have your neck straight — on a deep inhale, drop your chin to your chest gently. Exhale and return to the starting position. Repeat ten times.

3: Neck turn: Sitting or standing have your neck straight — tuck your chin slightly. On a deep inhale, turn your head to the left as far as it will gently go. Exhale and return to the starting position. Repeat to the right. Do ten of these neck stretches.

4: Side neck tilt: Sitting or standing have your neck straight — tuck your chin slightly. On a deep inhale, tilt your head so that you appear to bring your left ear to your left shoulder. Exhale and return to the starting position. Repeat to the right. Do ten of these neck stretches.

5: Lower back muscle stretch: Sit on the floor — bend the knees and have feet flat on the floor, about 18 inches apart. Contract abdominal muscles, tuck your chin to your chest and gently bend body toward the floor. Hold your shins or ankles with your hands for five seconds.

Breathe your cares and worry away.

Deep breathing is a powerful way to decrease stress and increase calm energy. It activates relaxation centers in the brain. When you are tense, your breathing is shallow. When you are emotionally distressed, your oxygen levels decrease. When you are angry or fearful, your breathing rate increases (normal breathing is about 16 times per minute). Poor body oxygenation can cause anxiety, depression, tight muscles, aches and pains and exacerbate chronic illness. When body fluid and congestion builds up, your breathing is probably restricted because breathing affects the circulation of lymph.

Breathing is controlled by two sets of nerves — the involuntary (autonomic) nervous system, and the voluntary nervous system. An imbalance of the autonomic nervous system contributes to health problems. Improving your breathing actually affects the autonomic nervous system and many of its involuntary functions.

Your body is an electromagnetic field of energy that operates at its own personal frequency or vibration. Deep breathing brings in energy and vitality. The way you breathe strengthens or depletes the vibration. Deep breathing enhances your energy field, feeding cells that make up the field. Oxygen causes your electromagnetic field to vibrate at a higher, more balanced rate.

Use your breathing as a stress release meditation:

1. Shift your focus away from your racing mind and your stressed emotions. There is a basic connection between your breath and your state of mind. Sit quietly and focus on your breath.

2. Consciously taking slow, deep, and regular breaths... your mind will become calm.

3. Recall a positive, pleasant past experience. Feel appreciation and thankfulness about the good things and people you have in your life. Shifting your focus to positive feelings helps neutralize the stress.

Breath and Body Stretch: Stand tall and raise your hands above your head. Stretch your arms and fingers as if you are reaching for the sky — pretend you are trying to climb up with your hands & arms. As you reach, inhale deeply through your nostrils while rising on your toes.

Exhale slowly, and gradually return to the starting position, with your arms hanging loosely at your side. Repeat this at least 5 times. This is a great warm-up to a brisk walk.

Filling a Balloon: Breathe in through the nose and imagine that the in-coming breath is filling a balloon in your belly, then continues up your torso and fills your entire upper body with air. After you are completely filled up with air, exhale, let go and feel the balloon emptying. Do a few of these deep breaths. Relaxation is just a breath away.

A Breathing Aid: Living Light Energies THE BREATH OF LIFE is a gemstone essence that uses the principles of vibrational medicine to aid breathing, support the respiratory system and the adrenals, reduce hyperactivity and increase vitality. It helps you breathe deeper.

Diaphragm breathing is the best for stress.

Diaphragmatic breathing is the deepest kind of breathing. It exercises the abdomen, diaphragm and all parts of the lungs ("rib cage" type of breathing exercises the chest muscles and middle parts of the lungs).

Deep diaphragm breathing lowers anxiety levels, relaxes and loosens muscles and generates a inner feeling of peace and calm. Deep, slow, diaphragm breathing oxygenates body tissues, stimulates brain cells, enhances memory capacity and energizes. Diaphragm breathing strengthens heart and lungs, encourages more restful sleep and slows the aging process.

Here are some basic diaphragm breathing steps:

1) Inhale deeply through your nose. Think about filling your lungs.

2) Exhale slowly through your mouth.

3) Continue breathing deeply for 30 seconds. It takes less than a minute to calm and center yourself during anxious moments. Breathing deeply for just one minute prevents the short, quick breaths which negatively affect the oxygen-carbon dioxide content of your blood.

4) Now breathe deeply to fill the lower part of your lungs. Your abdomen extends slightly as you fill it with air. Slowly exhale — your abdomen moves inward.

5) As you breathe in deeply, think of oxygen reaching and recharging all the cells of your body. As you exhale imagine all the stress and tension leaving your body.

Stress and Our Environment

Our world adds to our stress.

Environmental chemicals, toxins and contaminants add a harshness in our lives that's hard to ignore. Americans are exposed to all kinds of chemicals on an unprecedented scale. Industrial chemicals and their pollutant by-products, pesticides, additives in our foods, heavy metals, anesthetics, drug residues, and synthetic hormones are trapped in our bodies in greater concentrations than at any other point in history.

More than 2 million synthetic substances are known, 25,000 are added each year, and over 30,000 are produced on a commercial scale. Only a tiny fraction are ever tested for toxicity. The molecular structure of many chemical carcinogens interacts with human DNA, so long term exposure can result in metabolic and genetic alteration that affects cell growth, behavior and immune response. New research by the World Health Organization implicates toxic environmental chemicals in 60 to 80% of all cancers. Studies link pesticides and pollutants to hormone dysfunctions, psychological disorders, birth defects, still births and breast cancer. The wide variety of toxic substances means that every system of the body is affected — from deep level tissue damage to sensory deterioration.

As toxic matter saturates our tissues, antioxidants and minerals in vital body fluids are reduced, so immune defenses are thrown out of balance — eventually disease begins. Circumstances like this are the prime factor in today's immune compromised diseases like candidiasis, lupus, fibromyalgia, chronic fatigue syndrome, and cancer.

It sounds overwhelming. How can we avoid these health dangers if they are everywhere? There are two pathways I recommend...1) avoid and eliminate the harmful things you can; 2) detoxify your body several times a year to clean out the harmful things you can't avoid.

Almost everyone can benefit from a cleanse. It's one of the best ways to remain healthy in a destructive environment. Not one of us is immune to environmental toxins, and most of us can't escape to a remote, unpolluted habitat. In the last few decades we have become dangerously able to harm the health of our entire planet, even to the point of making it uninhabitable for life. We must develop further and take even larger steps... those of cooperation and support. Mankind and the Earth must work together — to save it all for us all. It starts with us. We can take positive steps to keep our own body systems in good working order so that toxins are eliminated quickly.

We can also take a closer look at our own air, water and food. We can read more labels and avoid highly chemicalized foods. We can buy fresh organically grown foods when they're available. We can avoid using toxic household products. Because of childhood accidents, many companies produce two versions of their products, an environmentally harmful one, and a safe alternative.

We can also keep a watchful eye on the politics that control our environment. Legislation on health and the environment follows two pathways in America today... the influence of business and profits, and the demands of the people for a healthy environment and responsible stewardship of the Earth.

Note: For detailed information on how to protect yourself from environmental chemicals, toxins and other contaminants, see *Detoxification - All you need to know to recharge, renew and rejuvenate your body, mind and spirit!* by Linda Page 1999.

Is your body becoming toxic?

Chemicals are polluting the earth's environment faster than the human organism can adapt to them. Toxins are building up and our bodies are becoming filters trapping the pollutants. The level of chemicals in our air, food and water supply alters us at the most basic level — our enzymes, then spreads throughout our systems to lower our threshold of resistance to disease.

Prolonged mental stress and negative emotions can create internal poisons. A fast foods diet, a severely unbalanced diet, or simply too much food overburden elimination systems. Lack of exercise contributes to toxicity, too. The body's natural cleansing cycle of oxygen and vital nutrients depends upon exercise. A stagnant system encourages toxic build-up.

Do you need to detox? Ask yourself these questions:

- Do you feel congested from too much food or the wrong kinds of food?
- Do you feel lethargic, like you need a good spring cleaning?
- Do you need to eliminate drug residues? Or normalize after illness or a hospital stay?
- Do you need a jump start for a healing program?
- Do you need a specific detox program for a serious health problem?
- Do you want to streamline your body processes for more energy?
- Do you need to remove toxins causing a health problem?
- Do you want to prevent disease? Or rest and rejuvenate your whole body?
- Do you want to assist weight loss? Do you want to clear up your skin?
- Do you want to slow aging and improve body flexibility?
- Do you want to improve your fertility?

Note: Laboratory tests like stool, urine, blood or liver function, and hair analysis can also shed light on the need for detoxification.

Body signs can tell you that you need to detoxify.

We all have different "toxic tolerance" levels. Listen to your body when it starts giving you those "cellular phone calls." If you can keep the amount of toxins in your system below your toxic level, your body can usually adapt and rid itself of them.

Do you have:

- Frequent, unexplained headaches or back or joint pain, or arthritis?
- Chronic respiratory problems, sinus problems or asthma?
- Abnormal body odor, bad breath or coated tongue?
- Food allergies, poor digestion or chronic constipation with intestinal bloating or gas?
- Brittle nails and hair, psoriasis, adult acne, or unexplained weight gain over 10 pounds?
- Unusually poor memory, chronic insomnia, depression, irritability, chronic fatigue?
- Environmental sensitivities, especially to odors?

Some of the harmful substances in our environment are EMFs (electromagnetic fields). We can't hear, smell, see, or touch them; we are exposed to them every day; they are directly related to sress. Learning about EMFs and taking steps to protect yourself can certainly reduce your exposure or at least strengthen your system during exposure. In the early nineteen seventies, research began to surface and create worrisome connections between EMFs and a number of serious health problems, including cancer. Because the connections affected so many business groups and so much technical development, there has been suppression of the facts about the potential health risks of EMFs. Today, little by little, due to the bold actions of a few concerned scientists, agency officials and health writers, the word about EMFs is finally getting out.

Electromagnetic fields generate radiation in the form of waves, which diminish as you move away from their source. (Fields from appliances disappear in a matter of a few feet; fields from transmission lines go for hundreds of feet.) Electric fields can be shielded — by houses, trees, etc., but magnetic fields are difficult to shield because they can pass through anything that doesn't contain a high degree of iron. This difference is important because it seems the dangers of electromagnetic fields come from their magnetic fields, not from exposure to the electric fields.

Dr. Robert Becker, M.D. has some astounding reports on the investigations of the connection between stress and EMFs. Some of the most upsetting show birth defects in laboratory animals exposed to weak EMF fields, decreased task performance in exposed animals, and changes in the blood composition of human subjects after EMF exposure (especially alterations in blood chemistry of men working on underground cables which produced strong electromagnetic fields).

World-wide research confirms many of Dr. Robert Becker's findings:
• Biochemical tests on rabbits found that exposing them to magnetic fields caused a generalized stress reaction marked by large amounts of cortisone in the bloodstream — the same response called forth by a prolonged stress.
• Cortisone levels in monkeys exposed to a 200 gauss field (a unit used for measuring magnetic fields) for four hours a day showed that their bodies had a marked stress response.
• Russian research found stress hormones released in rats exposed to microwaves, even if they were irradiated only briefly by minute amounts of energy.
• Russian and Polish research has established that after prolonged exposure to EMFs, the activation of the stress system changes to depression, indicating exhaustion of the adrenal cortex. One study reported hemorrhage and cell damage in the adrenal cortex from a month's exposure to a 50-hertz, 130 gauss magnetic field.
• Soviet studies of ELF magnetic fields (extremely low-frequency radiation) on the endocrine system show "slow" stress response and activation of the "fast" fight-or-flight hormones. The responses were triggered in rats in just *one day* and hormone levels didn't return to normal for up to two weeks. Insulin insufficiency and rise in blood sugar came from the same field.
• Naval Aerospace Medical Research at Pensacola, Florida has found slow stress response in rats from very weak electric fields, as low as five thousandths of a volt per centimeter. Their tests showed that when the fields vibrated in the ELF (extremely low-frequency radiation) range, they increased distress signal levels of the neurotransmitter acetylcholine in the brainstem, apparently subliminally, without the animal's becoming aware of it. The findings are highly worrisome to humans because the fields used were well within the background levels of a typical office where workers are regularly exposed to electric fields between a hundredth and a tenth of a volt per centimeter and magnetic fields between a hundredth and a tenth of a gauss.

Note 1: An impressive array of studies on the adverse health effects of EMFs has been collecting over the years. Reliable researchers report troubling findings about electromagnetic field exposure on tissues, cells and entire biological systems. See the bibliography, page 95 for more reading.

Note 2: Sage Associates Environmental Consultants, Montecito, CA offers a unique EMF monitoring service for people who wish to evaluate their EMF exposure. A small meter is worn for a week to determine your magnetic field exposure. The information is then downloaded and the results printed out for you. Sage Associates 805-969-0557.

Can we do anything to protect ourselves against EMF waves?

Antioxidants can help protect us from environmental chemicals, toxins, other various contaminants and EMFs.

We can reduce some exposure, especially by strengthening our bodies against free radical formation. Antioxidants are champion free radical fighters. Besides toxicity, chemical oxidation is the other process that allows disease. The oxygen that "rusts" and ages us also triggers free radical activity, a destructive cascade of incomplete molecules that damages DNA and other cell components. And if you didn't have a reason to reduce your animal fat intake before, here is a critical one: oxygen combines with animal fat in body storage cells and speeds up the free radical process. It is the oxidative damage done by free radicals which underlies many chronic illnesses. Antioxidants function by neutralizing the free radicals before they can do their damage. One of the most important attributes of antioxidants is to help prevent the damage to proteins (critical to healing) in the cell membranes.

Free radical formation is linked to environmental stressors.... and EMFs.

The common feature of all oxidative stress effects is the formation of free radicals. Free radicals are reactive oxygen atoms formed by the ordinary metabolic breakdown of organic compounds in our body. Your body takes 10,000 free radical hits a day just in normal, everyday living. Unfortunately it doesn't end there - free radicals can also be caused and accelerated by exposure to environmental pollutant contaminants like cigarette smoke, drugs, herbicides, pesticides, solvents, food chemicals, heavy metals, rancid oils, radiation and more.

EMF interaction with free radicals produces more free radicals, one of the mechanisms by which EMFs damage the body. Researchers theorize that certain types of rapid pulses EMFs may interfere with the normal activity of the pineal gland deep in the brain, blocking the release of a hormone called melatonin, a potent antioxidant. Many of us know melatonin's role in regulating our body clock, but melatonin also seems to suppress harmful tumor growth.

Why are free radicals bad?

Free radicals are oxygen atoms with an unpaired electron, an unbalanced state that drives the free radical to combine with other moleules. When a free radical combines with another molecule it destroys an enzyme, a protein molecule or a complete cell.

There are five types of free radical damage.

1: Damage to fat compounds — *reaction between oxygen and the fats in foods causes them to turn rancid. Rancid fats cannot be digested properly and they release free radicals.*

2: Cell membrane damage — *membranes of cells are composed of two different types fats (saturated and unsaturated), interspersed with protein molecules. Unsaturated fats in the cell membrane are especially susceptible to free radical damage.*

3: Lysosome damage — *lysosomes are cell membranes with special degrative enzymes. Free radicals can damage the lysosome membrane and spill the contained enzymes, causing cell damage.*

4: Accumulation of age pigment — *age pigment (lipofuscin) accumulation interferes with cell chemistry.*

5: Damage to protein structures — *includes damage to the protein in membranes, damage to nucleic acids (DNA/RNA), enzymes, neurotransmitters, etc.*

Antioxidants are premier protection in preventing free radical damage.

Even though our bodies produce the necessary antioxidants to deactivate normal free radical formation, we are so bombarded with additional environmental stressors it is unlikely that we receive sufficient antioxidants through our food to take care of nutritional needs *and* fight extra free radicals. I believe antioxidant supplements and herbs are necessary to bolster our antioxidant defense system.

Antioxidant nutrients protect against free radical damage risks like heart disease, cancer, Alzheimer's, arthritis, and chronic immune compromised diseases. Antioxidants slow down aging, fight infection and boost wound healing.

Antioxidants enhance each other; a combination of several antioxidants provides greater protection than any single antioxidant. When you choose a natural source antioxidant, it also acts synergistally with the antioxidant foods (fresh fruits and vegetables) in your diet. Look for an antioxidant supplement that includes plenty of carotenes, vitamin C complex with bioflavonoids, vitamin E with selenium and zinc, the amino acids cysteine, tyrosine and glutathione, coenzyme Q-10, pycnogenol and herbal antioxidants like ginkgo biloba, astragalus, garlic, turmeric, ginseng and green tea extract.

Here are some antioxidant combinations our group has tested and found effective:

- Crystal Star HERBAL ANTIOXIDANT CAPS
- Jarrow ANTIOXIDANT OPTIMIZER, ALPHA LIPOIC ACID, GINKGO BILOBA + GRAPE SEED
- Biotec Food CELL GUARD
- American Finest ANTIOXIDANT COMPLEX
- NutriCology ANTIOX FORMULA LL, COENZYME Q10 SOFTGELS, QUERCETIN 300 (a bioflavonoid which shows inhibition of cancer cell and leukemia cell proliferation; radioprotective, to reduce side effects during radiation therapy)
- Transformation Enzyme EXCELLZYME
- Enzymatic Therapy GREEN TEA ANTIOXIDANT
- Source Naturals COENZYME Q10 ULTRA POTENCY, PROANTHODYN
- Rainbow Light MULTI-CAROTENE ANTIOXIDANT SYSTEM
- Solgar ADVANCED ANTIOXIDANT FORMLA, ADULT CHEWABLE ANTIOXIDANT TABS
- Schiff PHYTOCHARGED ANTIOXIDANT BLEND
- Country Life SUPER 10 ANTIOXIDANT
- Futurebiotics OXY-SHIELD
- Prevail ANTIOXIDANTS

Stress and Your Heart

Chronic stress attacks your entire cardiovascular system. High blood pressure, irregular heart-

beat and congestive heart failure are cause coronary arteries to constrict walls. A high stress lifestyle along with you on a direct pathway to a heart at- knew about type A personalities and is still the number one killer of Ameri- 550,000 women will die of heart dis- all tied to stress. Stress reactions and cholesterol to build on artery bottled up anger or grief can put tack. Even ancient Greek physicians apoplexy! Cardiovascular disease cans. Over 450,000 men and ease this year.

There's more you should know...

Until very recently, men and women's heart disease was considered largely the same. Most doctors I've talked to, even recently, don't know it or don't believe it, but I see big differences in men and women when it comes to the heart — in both the problems and the treatment. Over the last 20 years, I've worked extensively to create natural "heart healing" programs tailored for the unique heart needs of men and women.

Men's heart disease has been the only focus of conventional medicine for decades. Until 1995, women were largely left out of heart census taking.

Stress is a part of all three top cardiovascular problems men face:
—EMOTIONAL HEALTH: One of the most interesting things studies show about men is that although most men show little emotion, emotional health is a major factor in men's heart disease. Stress, anger and overwork are now, and probably always have been, the major triggers of heart attacks for men.

—HIGH BLOOD PRESSURE, often called "the silent killer," affects 1 in 3 of all U.S. adults. Men are more at risk for HBP than women until about age 55. When blood pressure is high, the heart and arteries are over-worked, and artery hardening speeds up. Coronary heart disease is almost 5 times more likely in people with high blood pressure!

—ATHEROSCLEROTIC PLAQUE restricts blood flow leading to heart attacks, strokes, even gangrene. It's strongly tied to a diet high in animal fats like butter, red meat, ice cream and eggs, the very foods many men overeat!

A Man's Healthy Heart Program

A man can carve out his own heart health with his knife and fork. My anti-stress diet on page 10 is perfect if you've got high stress levels and heart problems. It emphasizes all the heart healthy foods — fresh, whole fiber foods, high mineral foods with lots of potassium and magnesium, oxygen-rich foods from green vegetables, sprouts and wheat germ (wheat germ oil can raise the oxygen level of the heart as much as 30%) and vegetable proteins.

Special diet watchwords for men:

• Men tend to overeat fatty foods. A low fat diet has to be part of a man's heart protection plan. It is essential for recovery from existing heart problems. Reduce fatty dairy foods like ice cream and rich cheeses. Cut back on red meat, especially pork.

• Use olive oil instead. You can't fry in olive oil, but fried foods are so bad for your heart that this is probably a plus. Olive oil boosts healthy HDL cholesterol levels and removes blood fats.

• Men need more fiber! Fiber has proven in numerous studies to reduce arterial plaque from atherosclerosis. Herbs are a good source of cleansing fiber for the male system. Herbs also help reduce cholesterol and eliminate fatty build-up, too. I recommend an herbal fiber rich drink mix like Crystal Star's CHOL-LO FIBER TONE™ (with *oat bran, flax seed, psyllium husks, guar gum, apple pectin, acidophilus, fennel seed, heartsease and vitamin E*).

• Add spices like garlic, onions, tumeric and cayenne peppers to your diet. Hundreds of clinical tests show garlic and onion's phytochemicals help keep blood flowing, reduce blood pressure and serum cholesterol and the build-up of arterial plaque. Cayenne peppers enhance cardiovascular health, dilate arteries and reduce blood pressure. Tumeric, an anti-inflammatory spice, helps decrease cholesterol levels and prevents progression of atherosclerosis.

An herbal formula like Crystal Star HEARTSEASE CIRCU-CLEANSE™ TEA (*with bilberry, kukicha, ginger root, hawthorn, ginkgo biloba, licorice, astragalus and peppermint*) has other herbs that boost circulation and thin "sticky blood."

• Eat more SUPERGREEN foods, especially spinach and chard, for magnesium therapy. A magnesium deficiency can contribute to hypertension, irregular heartbeat, even heart failure!

• Eat seafood at least once a week. An 11 year study covering over 22,000 male physicians found that eating seafood just once a week cuts men's risk of sudden cardiac death by 52%!

• Eat vitamin C rich foods like citrus fruits, broccoli or peppers. Low levels of vitamin C are linked to pregressive atherosclerosis and increased risk of heart attack. A new study shows that men with no pre-existing heart disease, but deficient in vitamin C have 3.5 times MORE heart attacks than men who get enough vitamin C.

• Wine relieves stress. Studies show that just drinking 1-2 glasses of wine each day cuts risk for coronary heart disease by 50%! New research reveals that resveratrol in red wine reduces even blood clotting in arteries narrowed by years of heavy fat consumption.

• Herbal stress busters work for men to reduce anxiety linked to high blood pressure. Herbal nervines like *kava kava, passsionflower and scullcap* calm and soothe acute stress reactions.

—For a man's chronic stress, *Siberian ginseng* builds the body's resistance to stress and restores nervous system health.

Two excellent therapies for men:

1: Oral chelation can help reverse men's heart disease. Although intravenous chelation with EDTA has largely been ignored by mainstream medicine, it has been used successfully for over 40 years for blood vessel diseases such as arteriosclerosis. (Intravenous chelation with EDTA (ethylenediamine tetra acetic acid, a synthetic amino acid) binds to and flushes out arterial plaque deposits that cause hardening of the arteries. It's a powerful therapy, but it's very expensive.) Oral chelation is a good option for men. It's much cheaper and more convenient than IV chelation, yet still improves blood flow and may even reverse some cardiovascular problems.

Oral chelation formulas with EDTA are available over-the-counter. Consider Golden Pride's FORMULA #1 561-640-5700.

2: Believe it or not, donating blood regularly can prevent a heart attack for a man! Men have twice as much iron in their bodies as women. Iron acts as a catalyst in cholesterol oxidation, linked to hardening and scarring of the arteries. A recent study finds that men cut their risk for heart attack or stroke by up to a third by reducing their excess iron when they regularly donate blood. Everybody wins.

What about heart disease in women?

A heart attack is especially serious for a woman. Statistics show that a woman is 50% MORE likely to die from a heart attack than a man! Last year, almost 550,000 American women died from cardiovascular disease — over 100,000 more deaths than men! Heart disease deaths accounted for more than 54%, over half, of all female deaths! Even more frightening, women receive less medical treatment despite having more cardiac symptoms than men.

What are the biggest heart problems for women?

Heart disease for women is linked to high cholesterol, obesity or too little exercise as it is in men. It is also clearly hormone-related. There is no time that a woman's risk for heart disease is higher than during menopause. Risk for heart disease rises noticeably with every year a woman approaches menopause and continues to rise with age. It's why hundreds of thousands of new, prophylactic, hormone replacement therapy prescriptions are written every year by doctors trying to protect menopausal women from heart disease.

Heart disease may be more dangerous for women than for men.

—Women have heart attacks at older ages when they are in poorer health than men.

—Female arteries are less able to compensate for the partial death of heart muscle caused by a heart attack, so a second heart attack is more dangerous.

Heart attack symptoms are also different. Women are less likely to have intense chest pains during a heart attack.

In addition to the normal symptoms of:
—Chest pressure or pain in the center of the chest for several minutes
—Numbness spreading to the face, neck or arms, usually on one side
—Chest pain with severe headache, light-headedness, sweating or nausea
—Dimness or loss of vision, especially in one eye
—Trouble talking or understanding speech
—Sudden severe headache and dizziness, leading to unsteadiness or a sudden fall

Women experiencing a heart attack may also have:
—Shortness of breath
—Sudden fatigue
—Unexplained back pain

Are you having a panic attack or a heart attack?

Stress can cause a panic attack that feels a lot like a heart attack. Many women confuse panic attacks with heart attacks during menopause because their symptoms seem so severe. Menopausal heart palpitations and nighttime anxiety attacks are extremely common. They appear to be a direct result of fluctuating hormones. When I first went into menopause, I remember waking up terrified that I was having a heart attack, but found out later it was a panic attack.

Panic attack signs to look for:
—hyperventilating or feeling short of breath, especially at night
—racing heartbeat, dizziness or feeling faint
—bolting upright out of bed in the early morning hours
—feeling like you're "going crazy" or losing control
—being full of fear that has no basis in reality

If you have these symptoms, you're probably suffering from a panic attack. It will more than likely pass quickly. If symptoms persist, seek out a qualified health practitioner. Herbs offer relief from nighttime panic attacks. Cardiotonic herbs de-stress your cardiovascular system, reduce heart attack risk and relieve palpitations. I keep Crystal Star "HEART STABILIZER FOR WOMEN" extract with *hawthorn, arjuna, ashwagandha* and *passionflowers* by my bed for immediate relief.

Another option: GABA, 750 to 1000mg daily or as needed during an attack, mimics valium effects without sedation.

Can you prevent panic attacks? Start with your diet.

—Avoid anxiety culprits: caffeine (and over-the-counter drugs containing caffeine), sugar, foods with colorings, fast and fried foods, preserved meats like lunch meats and alcohol.
—Add comfort foods during the day: brown rice, mashed potatoes, yogurt, oatmeal, and steamed vegetables. If you drink milk, switch to goat's milk instead of cow's milk.
—Make sure your diet contains:
  • Foods rich in calcium for stress relief and immune response, like sesame seeds, almonds, soy foods, low fat dairy foods, and dark, leafy greens.

•Foods rich in magnesium to protect your nerves, like sea plants, wheat germ and bran, most nuts and soy foods.

•Foods rich in B vitamins to support your adrenals, like nutritional yeast, brown rice, nuts and beans.

•Foods rich in vitamin C for more active stress response, like hot and sweet peppers, leafy greens, broccoli, kiwi, and citrus fruits.

Take some calming, soothing herbs during the day: try a kava combination. Kava is a proven anxiety reliever and actually enhances brain function. Crystal Star RELAX CAPS™ (with *ashwagandha, black cohosh, scullcap, kava kava, black haw, hops, valerian, Eur. mistletoe, wood betony, lobelia and oatstraw*) or Crystal Star STRESSED OUT™ tea (with *chamomile, rosemary, catnip, feverfew, heartsease, white willow, gotu kola, wood betony, blessed thistle, stevia*).

Panic preventing supplements: before bed- Cal/Mag/Zinc, 4 capsules and B-Complex 100mg. Between meals L-Tyrosine 500mg morning and evening.

Lifestyle tips for panic attacks occurring between 3 to 5 o'clock in the morning...

—Get out of bed, turn on a TV show, take a shower, see the sun rising and life going on. Get dressed and walk outside.

—Do some stretches, or a little mild exercise or walk your dog. There is a body chemical basis for fear, released through hormones. Exercise oxygenates and replaces that function.

—Think positive. Review a recent success, remind yourself of your talents and abilities.

—Realize that you are not alone, no matter what situation you find yourself in or what mistakes you have made.

—Remind yourself never to let outside worries make you violent toward those you love, or against yourself, for instance, through a heart attack.

—No matter what it is, it will pass.

Can Herbs Help In An Emergency Heart Attack?

Sometimes they can. Up through the nineteenth century, tincture of cayenne was a traditional healer's emergency method to bring a person out of a heart attack. About 5 dropperfuls (approx. 30 drops each) have been able to stop a heart attack. If the victim is unconscious, begin with two dropperfuls and add more as response begins. Up to 10 or 12 droppersful may be needed, but reports from healers even today are sometimes miraculous for this technique.

When taken at the onset of symptoms, the amino acid L-Carnitine, 330mg. 3x daily, lessens the severity of a heart attack and reduces complications in the weeks following. Stronger, liquid carnitine can sometimes be used in an emergency. Ask your health practitioner.

A heart attack is an emergency! Modern medicine is at its best in just this kind of emergency. If you live near a clinic of any kind, get there immediately if you or someone close to you is having a heart attack. A heart attack or stroke does most of its damage in the first six hours.

Congestive heart failure is another big cardiovascular problem for menopausal women. Over two million women alive today have CHF. Congestive heart failure occurs when the heart is unable to efficiently pump blood. In people with CHF, risk for sudden cardiac arrest and death is 6-9 times higher than the general population!

Here are the congestive heart failure symptoms to watch for:
—Extreme fatigue
—High iron stores after menopause
—Unusual water retention (particularly bloated ankles)

A daily herbal heart tonic can help protect you as heart, circulatory and immune support against CHF. Crystal Star's "HEART PROTECTOR FOR WOMEN," (with *hawthorn, motherwort, ashwagandha, dong quai, ginkgo biloba, night blooming cereus, arjuna, juniper berries, poria cocos, red sage, scullcap, valerian and ginger root).*
—*Hawthorn* protects and strengthens the whole vascular system. Hawthorn is especially good if you have a weak heart because it eases stress on your heart.
—*Arjuna*, an antioxidant Ayurvedic herb, regulates blood pressure and supports the health of the heart muscle so it can pump blood better.
—*Ginger's* anti-clotting properties make it an effective and, in my mind, much better long term protector for your heart than aspirin against heart attacks and strokes. Use ginger regularly in cooking. Crystallized ginger is fine, too.

New studies find women with Atrial Fibrillation, an irregular heartbeat, are 90% more likely to die than those without. It's one of the newest heart dangers for menopausal women. A cardiotonic, herbal heart protector with *arjuna and hawthorn* can help regulate heartbeat and strengthen your entire cardiovascular system.

Finally, women need to know how to lower high Homocysteine levels.
Women with high homocysteine levels and low folic acid in their blood are TWICE as likely to have a heart attack as women with normal levels. Women are at risk for higher homocysteine levels around the time of menopause. (Elderly people with vitamin B deficiencies are also more at risk for higher homocysteine levels.) But you can lower homocysteine levels naturally. A simple 4 point program shows protective results for women in just a few months.

1: B vitamins can come to your rescue. A new study shows that higher intake of folic acid and vitamin B-6 lowers risk for cardiovascular disease in women almost 50%. I recommend B-Complex 100mg daily, with 50mg extra B-6, 400mcg extra of folic acid and 1000mcg B-12, as cofactors to help break down homocysteine.

2: Four garlic capsules (about 1200mg a day) also help maintain aortic elasticity.

3: Daily ginger helps prevent blood "stickiness." I eat ginger every day in one form or another — pickled, crystallized fresh, dried, extract, capsules, even adding a little GINGER WONDER syrup (New Chapter) to make real ginger-ale are all effective.

4: Red wine, one glass with dinner. Red wine contains resveratrol which has phytoestrogenic, antioxidant and anti-coagulant properties to help protect women from cardiovascular disease after menopause.

Reducing homocysteine levels with TMG (trimethylglycine).

Homocysteine is created in the body from the metabolism of methionine, an essential amino acid. A healthy person's metabolism converts excess homocysteine back into methionine naturally. But if your diet is high in fat and sugar, and low in vegetables and whole grains, or if you smoke, the metabolism loop that keeps your blood homocysteine normal is disrupted.

New tests show even more about homocysteine. While high homocysteine levels in blood increase the risk for heart disease in both men and women, high homocysteine levels in spinal fluid are associated with fibromyalgia and chronic fatigue, a particular problem for women. TMG (trimethylglycine), naturally found in beets, leafy green vegetables and legumes, is a nutrient involved in the natural homocysteine metabolism process.

Consider NutriCology HOMOCYSTEINE METABOLITE FORMULA or Natural Balance CARDIO-TMG to supplement your TMG.

Stress and Poor Digestion

Has stress gotten to your tummy? Your body tells you in a variety of unpleasant ways that you are under stress — all the way from "butterflies" in your stomach to nausea to a full-blown, bleeding ulcer. Stress has an equal, if not more dramatic effect on digestive health even than your diet. Don't let it get that far.

Stress states like fear, worry, anger, nervousness or strong emotion, all cause impaired digestive functions, usually for several hours - especially in men. Gastrointestinal peristalsis is inhibited. Food isn't metabolized properly. If you're getting distressed digestion warning signals, like gas, heartburn, nausea, heaviness, cramps or after-meal headaches, try eating when you are more relaxed, and end your meal with a warm, mint-based digestive tea, or Crystal Star STRESSED OUT TEA™ (with *chamomile, rosemary, peppermint, catnip, feverfew, heartsease, gotu kola, white willow, wood betony, blessed thistle*).

Enzymes are champion stress-fighters for indigestion.

When you're under stress your enzyme flow is suppressed. Eating under stress means that the proper enzymes may not come into play at the right time for the right food. Your body's acid-alkaline balance gets out of whack. Men seem to be particularly at risk for digestion stress reactions. Men tend to overeat and eat junk "comfort foods" when they're under stress. They get far more heartburn than women (a clear sign of low enzyme activity). Most men benefit greatly when they add herbal enzymes to their tension-fighting arsenal. Crystal Star AFTER MEAL ENZ™ EXTRACT (with *peppermint, spearmint, orange and lemon mints, papaya, licorice, hibiscus*).

Here are some tried and true plant enzyme products for men: Transformation DIGESTZYME, Herbal Products and Development POWER-PLUS ENZYMES, and Sonne's No. 6 PRO-GEST; and two for women: Rainbow Light ADVANCED ENZYME SYSTEM and Prevail DIGESTION FORMULA.

If it's looking like you have a stress ulcer... Licorice root is a favorite herb of mine for protecting the digestive system from damage caused by stress. Healing response in clinical tests is outstanding for both chronic duodenal, and acute gastric ulcers. Rather than suppressing acid release into the stomach as most drugs do, an herbal digestive formula containing licorice encourages normal immune defenses that prevent ulcer formation. Licorice helps protect a healthy mucosal lining in the intestinal tract, and may be taken as needed to soothe burning and the pain of inflammation. Used over a two to three month period, a licorice ulcer compound is effective in rebuilding healthy gastrointestinal tissue and providing enzyme therapy for better food use.

—Crystal Star U.L.C.R.™ Complex Caps (with *goldenseal, licorice, slippery elm, myrrh, capsicum, calendula, bilberry*) helps re-establish gastrointestinal balance and healthy mucosal lining.

—Crystal Star Ginseng-Licorice Elixir™ also inhibits the *H. pylori* stomach bacterium that causes most ulcers.

Stress and Migraine Headaches

It's the stess headache of the 21st century. Almost twenty percent of American men and thirty percent of women experience migraines as part of their stress reactions. A migraine is the end result of all the other stress emotions.... anger and frustration, anxiety, nerves, fear, grief, disappointment, etc.

Low serotonin levels (see page 23), excess alcohol (especially red wine), food chemicals (like nitrates, MSG, nitroglycerin), withdrawal from caffeine or other drugs (constrict blood vessels), and computor eyestrain are other body stress facts of modern life that also trigger migraine headaches.

Migraines have been considered a vascular headache because they involve an instability of blood vessels, usually excessive dilation of blood vessels in the head.

For most people, the pain seems like it's in the brain, a throbbing, pounding sharp pain that makes the sufferer's head feel like it's about to explode. But the brain does not contain sensory nerves (brain operations in ancient times were done without anesthesia). The pain center actually resides outside of the brain, in the lining of the brain and the scalp.

Are natural pain relievers strong enough to handle migraines?

Chemical painkilling drugs, though strong, still only mask pain or deaden certain body nerve mechanisms so that they cannot function. 5-HT1 receptor agonists are new anti-migraine drugs that act on serotonin receptors on the blood vessels on the spinal cord and brain. Yet they have wide-ranging side effects — chest pain (sometimes severe angina, heart arrhythmias, even heart attacks), dizziness, lethargy and drowsiness, blood pressure changes (hypertensive reactions), nausea, vomiting and seizures.

Herbal pain relievers are more subtle and work at a deeper level — to relax, soothe, ease and calm. Natural pain relievers allow you to use pain for information about your body, yet not be overwhelmed by the trauma to body and spirit that unrelieved suffering can bring.

Here are some migraine preventers and pain-relievers:

—Massage the temple and back of the neck. Because migraines are connected to vascular instability, the blood vessels of the temple are visibly dilated. Relief can often be felt by local compression of these blood vessels or the main artery of the neck.

—Get oxygen — take a brisk walk or try breathing deeply. The more oxygen available to the brain, the fewer headaches there will be.

Some herbal analgesics are effective for migraines. I have often heard the comment that "herbs work when nothing else will." Feverfew is often used in herbal migraine formulas. It's an old headache remedy, and modern studies on one of its active components (*parthenolide*) show it decreases the frequency and intensity of migraine attacks. It works by inhibiting the release of blood vessel dilating chemicals in plasma platelets, inhibiting inflammatory histamines and restoring proper blood vessel tone.

Herbal products specifically targeted for migraine headaches. Crystal Star Migr-Ease™ Caps (with *feverfew, valerian, wild lettuce, rosemary, catnip, European mistletoe, gentian and licorice*).
• Crystal Star Migr.™ Tea (with *feverfew, valerian, wild lettuce, ashwagandha, ginkgo biloba, cardamom and ginger.*)
• Herbs Etc. Migra Free (with *feverfew, periwinkle, ginkgo biloba, meadowsweet, white willow and stevia*) has 400mcg of Parthenolide per ml., an amount proven effective in clinical trials to stop migraine headache attacks, also helps prevent inflammation of blood vessels in the brain and may even help migraine headache attacks resistant to conventional medicines.
• Now Head Relief Liquid Extract (with *wildcrafted white willow bark, clematis, organically grown feverfew, meadowsweet, and fresh ginger*).

Stress and Your Immune Response

Has stress put your immune system under attack? The best way for our bodies to deal with chronic stress is to have a strong immune response. If your immune system has become a victim of stress, you're probably getting immune-compromised syndromes like chronic infections, colds, allergies or candida yeast overgrowth.

Are your adrenals always fighting a rear guard action?

Adrenal health is crucial to good immune response. Chronic stress means our adrenal glands have to constantly react and fight to defend our health. Like any soldier that's on the front lines 24 hours a day, the adrenals become exhausted. They lose the ability to recover and we lose the ability to fight off illness. First-sign conditions like low blood pressure, lethargy, mental spaciness, respiratory problems and chronic constipation set in. We get brittle nails, dry skin, cracked heels, puffy ankles and eyelids, PMS, brown spots on the skin, frail nerves and sparse body hair. We don't absorb our daily nutrition well because the adrenals help to synthesize cholesterol. We gain weight because the adrenals influence our metabolism of carbohydrates and sugars.

Herbs to the rescue for your adrenals! Certain herbs are adrenal tonics for better energy use. A well-crafted formula provides adrenal support and nourishment without adding stimulants or raw animal glandular tissue. Herbs for the adrenals encourage adrenal cortex secretion. A formula like Crystal Star ADRN-ACTIVE™ CAPS (with *licorice root, sarsaparilla, bladderwrack, uva ursi, Irish moss, ginger, astragalus root, capsicum and rose hips*) also helps regulate metabolic activity and controls histamine reactions if you have allergy or asthma.

Adrenal support formulas work at their best when taken with mineral-rich herbs that help restore overall strength to muscles and tissues. Over the years, we have recommended and seen good results with the following example of this kind of body rebuilding combination.

Note: Men seem to benefit more when they use Crystal Star ADRN™ EXTRACT (with *licorice, sarsaparilla, bladderwrack, Irish moss*) with the body rebuilding formula. Women report better results from the adrenal capsule/body rebuilder combination. Crystal Star BODY RE-BUILDER™ CAPS (with *spirulina, bee pollen, alfalfa, hawthorn, chlorella, barley grass, Siberian ginseng, carrot, sarsaparilla, red raspberry, kelp, wild cherry, rose hips, goldenseal and mullein*).

Tonic herbs are my first choice as over all immune boosters. Adaptogen herbs help the body handle stress, renew vitality, relieve fatigue and heighten resistance. Ginsengs of all kinds, as premier tonic adaptogens are some of the best immune stimulators. A combination like Crystal Star GINSENG SIX SUPER™ TEA (with *prince, American, Chinese and Siberian ginsengs, suma, tienchi, aralia, reishi, ginger, astragalus, St. John's wort and echinacea*) shows excellent results in restoring immune defenses. Most people notice a difference in one to two months.

An immune stengthening formula like Crystal Star SYSTEMS STRENGTH™ (with *barley, alfalfa, chlorella, borage, Siberian ginseng, dandelion, parsley, bilberry, schizandra, sea plants, licorice, nettles, horsetail, cranberry and fennel*) relies on brown rice and miso for building blocks. It balances body pH, regulates fluid osmosis and electrical activity, and aids digestion and regularity. It is a rich chlorophyll source, with large amounts of plant carotenes, B vitamins, essential fatty acids and octacosanal for tissue oxygen. It is a vigorous source of usable proteins and amino acids, and has almost twice the amount of protein as a comparable amount of wheat germ.

Here's my tried and true 8 step program to boost immune response against stress:

1: Take a high potency, concentrated, green, "superfood" like chlorella, barley grass, spirulina, alfalfa, etc. twice a week. The composition of chlorophyll is very similar to that of human plasma, so these foods provide something akin to a "mini-transfusion" for your bloodstream.

2: Include sea vegetables, like kelp, dulse, kombu or wakame in your diet for their therapeutic iodine, high potassium, and sodium alginate content.

3: Take a high potency lactobacillus or acidophilus complex, for friendly gastrointestinal flora and good food assimilation.

4: Balanced blood sugar is a key for adrenal gland recovery; get good vegetable protein every day from foods like brown rice and miso, with frequent small meals to keep your blood sugar up.

5: Aerobic exercise keeps circulation flowing and system oxygen high. Disease does not readily overrun a body where oxygen and organic minerals are high in the vital fluids.

6: Get 15 minutes of early morning sunlight every day to stimulate immunity. (Avoid excessive sun. Sun burn depresses immunity.)

7: Laugh. Laughter lifts more than your spirits. It also boosts the immune system. Laughter decreases cortisol, an immune suppressor, allowing immune boosters to function better.

8: Take a daily antioxidant supplement. Make sure it includes nutrients like vitamin E with selenium, beta carotene, zinc, CoQ-10, pycnogenol and vitamin C to protect against free radical damage. Check for herbs with strong antioxidant qualities — like *echinacea, chaparral, goldenseal root, Siberian ginseng, rosemary, astragalus, suma, burdock and pau d' arco.*

Here are some supplements I recommend:

—Allergy Research Group MYCOSTAT - six important immune mushrooms.

—Herbs Etc. DEEP CHI BUILDER - An immune system toner with *reishi* and *shiitake*.

—Transformation PUREZYME protease - a powerful immune booster.

Stress and Addictions Go Hand In Hand

We Americans have an expensive river of chemicals coursing through our national veins. We take some $19 billion worth of prescription drugs each year - 85 million aspirin every single day alone! Ten million Americans are officially classified as addicted to alcohol. At a cost to taxpayers of $276 billion dollars a year, some believe that it's the nation's number one health problem. The use of "hard" or "pleasure" drugs in today's society is also prevalent. Still, experts believe that the most serious addictions are those to pharmaceutical drugs. More than one million people a year (3 to 5 percent of admissions) end up in hospitals as a result of negative reactions to prescription drugs.

Clearly, modern drugs play lifesaving roles in emergency situations and they can help numerous health problems, especially short term, but most people begin taking drugs to alleviate boredom and fatigue, or to relieve physical or psychological pain. A detox program helps enormously to release drugs and alcohol from your system, but withdrawing after long time use can produce harsh effects (see following page). Drug detoxification is a process of releasing the stored substances while at the same time changing lifestyle habits so that you are no longer dependent on them. It is critical to fortify your body enough to give it the power to resist returning to the addictive substance. I highly recommend the supervision of a qualified health professional for an addictions cleanse, especially if the dependency has been long term and if the substance is highly addictive. (See DETOXIFICATION by Linda Page.)

Alcohol and drugs contribute to the stress response.

The symptoms that drugs or excessive alcohol address are merely the warning signs of deeper internal imbalances. Alcohol abuse especially may be brought on and marked by stress and depression. Drug use and drug therapy rarely fix anything. Drugs and alcohol can even aggravate an original health problem and add to the poisons in your body. All drugs are powerful, many drugs are dangerous, and many have been found to be ineffective in curing the condition for which they were prescribed and used for.

America's high stress lifestyles deplete energy reserves, motivating quick "high voltage fixes" to boost energy and relieve tension or boredom. Using drugs, alcohol, nicotine or caffeine to fuel your body's energy creates multiple deficiencies of essential nutrients like vitamins, minerals, essential fatty acids, amino acids and enzymes. The depletion sets off a chain reaction of more stress and more cravings. It's a vicious circle — a futile effort to satisfy increasing need and addiction eventually occurs.

For most people, this is just the beginning. Drugs regularly compromise immune response leading to hypothyroidism, chronic fatigue syndrome, and auto-immune diseases like mononucleosis, hepatitis, and chronic bronchitis. Even if serious disorders are avoided, consequences of drug overload are high. People who use a lot of drugs are always either sick or coming down with something. As soon as one cold, sore throat, bout of flu, or bladder infection is treated, a new one takes its place. Work is impaired, job time is lost, family and social life is affected and stress levels increase.

Okay, you've decided to get the chemicals out of your system and give natural energy sources a try. What about withdrawal? Can herbs and supplements make it any easier?

There's no doubt about it. The initial phase of drug withdrawal can be the most difficult part of your detox decision. It can last from a day or two to a week or more. Breaking destructive habits is hard. Your body reacts when a substance it thinks it depends on is removed. Withdrawal symptoms are the same as addiction symptoms, only worse and more frequent.

What does it feel like to withdraw from drugs or alcohol? You'll start getting chronic headaches, usually with diarrhea as your body tries to release toxins faster — and a lot of irritability. Some people experience hallucinations, disorientation or irrational thinking. Some go into depression. You'll probably sleep poorly, and your sleep may be interrupted during the night. Most people in withdrawal are sensitive to light and noise, hot and cold, and sweating.

I've worked with many people on this road. Here are some of the best watchwords I know:
—Look at each episode of discomfort as a little victory on the road to recovery.
—Every single day gets easier as more toxins are eliminated. As your body dislodges more toxins day by day, you have the satisfaction of knowing they are gone for good.
—One of the laws of the universe is that we don't have to fight the same battle twice.

One of the best things I've found to help yourself resist going back to an addiction is to fortify your body with nutrients. Eat an *optimally* healthful diet, take extra herbs and nutritional supplements. A well nourished body brings forth a sense of well being and strength which helps to melt the urges and desires you're trying hard to leave behind.

Here are some signs to look for as your body responds to your detox program cleanse:
—Your mood lifts as your nerves heal.
—Memory and thinking improve. (*Ginkgo biloba* extract helps speed brain processes up.)
—Your skin becomes clearer— less muddy; your eyes become brighter.
—Digestion for most people improves right away.
—Your immune response noticeably improves, usually within a month.

The overwhelming majority of addictive substance users suffer from nutrient deficiencies and metabolic imbalances. When these conditions are corrected, the need to get high by artificial means is sharply diminished. So wholesome nutritional support is an essential key to recovery from addictions. Give yourself plenty of time for regeneration. It may take up to a year to clear drugs from your bloodstream.

Purify your blood first to overcome addictions.

Overcoming addictions and alcohol abuse is far more successful when treatment is begun with a blood purifying cleanse. Follow-up studies show that as many as 75% of patients are still sober after one year when they start with a detoxification program.

The following "supernutrient" diet not only helps purify toxic blood, but helps rebuild a nutrient-depleted system. It is rich in vegetable proteins, high in minerals (especially magnesium for nerve stress), with Omega-3 oils, vitamin B and C source foods, and antioxidants.

Addictions Detox Diet

—On rising: a superfood/aloe drink gives energy and controls morning blood sugar drop: add 1 tsp. *each* to aloe vera juice: spirulina, bee pollen granules, brewer's yeast; or use 1 TB. of a superfood mix: Crystal Star Energy Green™; Arise & Shine Power Up; Green Foods Green Magma.

—Breakfast: make a mineral mix - 1 tsp. each: sesame seeds, wheat germ, bee pollen granules, brewer's yeast. Add to fresh fruit with yogurt; oatmeal or rice pilaf with maple syrup; or whole grain cereal or granola with apple juice.

—Mid-morning: have fresh carrot juice or Super V-7 veggie juice: 2 carrots, 2 tomatoes, handful each spinach and parsley, 2 celery ribs, $1/2$ cucumber, $1/2$ bell pepper. Add 1 TB. green superfood - Crystal Star Energy Green™ Drink; Transitions Easy Greens.

—Lunch: have a fresh "magnesium" dark greens salad topped with almonds or sunflower seeds. Snip on sea vegetables, 1 tsp. nutritional yeast, 1 tsp. flax or olive oil, 1 tsp. lemon juice and Bragg's Liquid Aminos.

—Mid-afternoon: have a glass of carrot juice with 1 TB. green superfood (see above); or Crystal Star Systems Strength™, or a ginseng restorative tea.

—Dinner: have brown rice and steamed vegetables with chopped onions, nutritional yeast and snipped shiitake mushrooms.

—Before Bed: have a cup of miso soup with 1 TB. sea vegetables and 1 tsp. pickled ginger.

For your ongoing diet:

• Eat magnesium-rich foods — green leafy and yellow vegetables, citrus fruits, whole grain cereals, fish and legumes.

• Eat potassium-rich foods — oranges, broccoli, green peppers, seafoods, sea vegetables, bananas and tomatoes.

• Eat chromium-rich foods — brewer's yeast, mushrooms, whole grains, sea foods and peas.

• Eat some vegetable protein at every meal.

• Alkalize, alkalize, alkalize. Cravings and withdrawal symptoms intensify when your body is over-acid. Foods that contribute to acidity are meats, dairy products, white flour foods and white sugars. Keep these foods at a minimum. Alkalizing foods are fruits and vegetables, juices, soups, seafoods and sea vegetables — even water.

Herbs help overcome addictions because they enhance your body's effort to cleanse itself.

Clean out toxins:
—Clean your lymph system with Echinacea Extract drops.

—Clean up cellular debris from drugs with Transformation Enzyme Purezyme.

—Liver support is the key to recovery from alcohol and drug abuse. Clean your liver with a liver flush tea such as Crystal Star Liv-Alive™ Tea (with *dandelion, watercress, yellow dock rt., pau d'arco, hyssop, parsley, Oregon grape rt., red sage, licorice, milk thistle sd., hibiscus, white sage*).

Note: *Goldenseal root* also stimulates the liver in its detoxification duties - goldenseal alkaloids help clear away toxicity. *Milk thistle seed* helps protect the liver from toxins.

Strengthen your adrenals:
—Crystal Star Adrn-Active™ Caps (with *licorice, sarsaparilla, bladderwrack, uva ursi, Irish moss, ginger, astragalus, capsicum, rose hips, ascorbate vit. C*).

Strengthen your nerves:
A complex broad spectrum herbal nervine helps you "get over the hump" and control many of the problems faced during withdrawal from drugs or alcohol. Crystal Star Withdrawal Support™ Caps (with *scullcap, gotu kola, Siberian ginseng, ascorbate vitamin C, kava kava, valerian, alfalfa, wood betony, licorice, capsicum*) is designed to depress craving, overcome nervous tension and low energy, help rebuild damaged nerve structure, encourage restful sleep, soothe withdrawal headaches and increase attention span and focus.

—Add herb source minerals for stability; Crystal Star Mineral Spectrum™ Caps (with *parsley, nettles, yellow dock, watercress, alfalfa, Irish moss, barley grass, dandelion, kelp, borage and dulse*).

Balance your system:
Use adaptogen/hormone balancing herbs like those found in Crystal Star Ginseng Six Super™ Tea (with *prince ginseng, kirin ginseng, echinacea angustifolia, pau d'arco, suma, astragalus, echinacea purpurea, St. John's wort, aralia, ashwagandha, Chinese white ginseng, Siberian ginseng, reishi mushroom, fennel, tienchi ginseng, ginger*).

—Ginseng is a key: Y.S. Royal Jelly/Ginseng Tea. Use Crystal Star Ginseng Six™ Energy Caps for drug addictions (with *bee pollen, Siberian ginseng, gotu kola, fo-ti, Chinese kirin ginseng, prince ginseng, suma, aralia, alfalfa, dong quai*).

—Aloe juice balances blood sugar, metabolism and hormonal system to help decrease cravings. AloeLife Terry's Herbal Aloe Detox Plus.

Energize:
Most people recovering from addictions find their energy levels are very low as the body tries to carry on without its usual "high voltage fix." Herbs can help you through the energy crunch. Crystal Star High-Energy™ Tea (with *gotu kola, peppermint, damiana, red clover, cloves, prince ginseng, kava kava, aralia, raspberry*) encourages better use of the body's own energy supply. It's an excellent "weaning" tea for withdrawal fatigue. It may be made and sipped throughout the day.

Supplements support your detoxification program:

• NutriCology Buffered C Powder (beet source) - 3 teaspoons daily. A study at the Haight-Ashbury Free Medical Clinic in San Francisco examined the effects of Buffered Ascorbate Compound (BAC) in the detox treatment of opiate and stimulant addiction. Two-thirds of the people in the study reported over 60% relief of acute withdrawal symptoms when taking BAC.

• Take antioxidants, like vitamins C, A and E, zinc and selenium. They bind with toxins and carry them out of the body: All One Multiple Vitamins, Minerals, Green Phyto Base. Amino acids, like L-cysteine, glutamine 500mg and tyrosine 500mg daily to help reduce cravings. Glutathione, formed in the body from L-cysteine, acts through detoxification enzymes to decrease the toxicity of most drugs and chemicals. Vitamin E strengthens adrenals and restores liver function.
—Jarrow Formulas Alpha Lipoic Acid or MRI Alpha-Lipoic Acid - among the most powerful liver detoxifiers ever discovered; Transformation Enzyme Excellzyme; Source Naturals Coenzyme Q_{10} Ultra Potency; Country Life Super 10 Antioxidant.

• Take kudzu caps. Tests on kudzu for alcohol abuse shows a reduction in alcohol intake.
—Planetary Formulas Kudzu caps.

• Take a full spectrum amino acid compound, 1000mg to rebuild from a low protein diet. L-cysteine and glutathione help decrease toxicity of many drugs and chemicals, reduce cravings.
—Allergy Research Thiodox.

• Take a mega potency Stress B Complex daily, 100-150mg. I like Nature's Secret Ultimate B.

Bodywork can shorten your healing time.

—Exercise: every day you can. Exercise helps move toxins out of your body, it reduces the stress of detoxing, it brings oxygen to your cells.

—Breathe deeply: Do deep breathing exercises on rising, and in the evening on retiring.

—Guided imagery: give your body some active encouragement. Actively imagine each gram of the addictive substance dislodging itself from your tissues, floating into your bloodstream and into your bladder or bowel for elimination. Make sure you visualize it leaving your body.

—Get a cleansing massage from a good massage therapist to help normalize your system. Take a hot sauna two or three times a week; or a sweating herbal bath such as Crystal Star Pounds Off™ Bath (with *jaborandi, thyme, angelica, elder, orange peel and blossoms, pennyroyal, kesu flower*).

—Hydrotherapy: alternating hot and cold showers are effective for muscle pain and cramping, circulation, bowel-bladder problems, body balance and energy. Begin with a comfortably hot shower for three minutes. Follow with a sudden change to cold water for 2 minutes. Repeat cycle three times, ending with cold. Follow with a brisk towel rub and mild stretching exercises.

Are You Addicted to Work?

Work addiction is becoming a stress sign of the millenium. Work addicts live in misery amid applause, slaps on the back, fat paychecks and performance awards.

A fallout of America's deficit spending eighties was that more than one member of a family had to work to keep the family at the same standard of living. Raising one's standard of living meant having to take on another job or extra work projects. Nineties families may have both husband and wife working two jobs, and teenage children working one or more jobs, too. The new millenium looks even harder in terms of work stress because American labor must compete with a global economy. It's easy to see how a workaholic lifestyle came into being and how work addiction insinuated itself into our society.

Fatigue is a nationwide epidemic. Every day, more tired legions of Americans fight to get out of bed and back into "the grind" of their working lives.
Why are we so exhausted? One of the biggest reasons is overwork. America is open for business 24 hours a day — and most of us are working most of those hours!

Don't confuse work addiction with hard work. Work addiction is when someone can't stop the process of work. They get into a "work mode" and they can't get out. They just keep going and going.... sometimes right to burnout and mental exhaustion. Even when they have to take a mandatory vacation, it takes them almost an entire time to forget about work and relax.
Most people can't keep it up for very long.

Work addiction can lead to chronic stress and

burnout. Stress and burnout cost the nation's employers an astounding $150 billion a year of medical expenses, absenteeism and low productivity! Burnout describes the exhaustion symptoms of work overload — low energy, chronic tiredness, daily headaches, upset stomachs, frequent colds and flu, achy muscles, lack of rest. If you're burnt out, you're probably feeling pretty negative about yourself, your job or your life. You may even be feeling hopeless or depressed (your colleagues may think you're on top of the world).

Are you addicted to work?

1: Is there a total lack of balance between work and other areas of your life? Work addicts don't feel like they are worth much unless they are working.

2: Do you overcommit on projects or obligations? Because of overcommitting, work addicts hardly ever think a project through before jumping into it, or finish the project on time.

3: Are your standards unrealistic? A work addict feels that nobody can do a job as well as they can. They delegate little, pile more on themselves under the guise of quality control.

4: Do you drive yourself (and your associates) mercilessly? Regardless of how much you actually work, do you tell yourself and everybody else that it is much more? Do you feel anxious and worthless when you aren't working? Any activity that isn't "productive" is a complete waste of time for a work addict. They have trouble letting go of work even when they aren't working, and tune out everything else while they think about work. A bizarre side effect: work addicts suffer "brown out amnesia" about conversations they had that weren't about work.

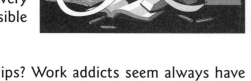

5: Most work addicts had strict, serious, puritanical up-bringings. They take themselves and their work very seriously with very little humor or acceptance of any fun. They're very responsible at getting work done but are not very responsible at all about other commitments.

6: Do you have a hard time with personal relationships? Work addicts seem always have their minds on work. Do you use work as a shield to avoid conflicts with yourself and your loved ones? Work addicts set standards of perfection for loved ones that are impossible to meet.

7: Are you constantly racing against the clock? Time is the most precious commodity for a work addict. They can't tolerate waiting....for anything. They get there fast but lose the details.

8: Does work get you "high?" Work addiction may be adrenaline addiction. Work addicts tend to turn every situation into crisis management to turn on the adrenaline high.

9: Do you have an obsessive sense of urgency? Work addicts are so over-extended their attention span is almost nil. Do you need immediate gratification for your efforts? The product is far more important to a work addict than the process. They rush a job through so that they can chalk up another notch on their accomplishments.

10: Can you see the forest for the trees? Work addicts are so wedded to their work that they often lose the ability to make good judgements about it — work conditions, fairness, salary, advancement. They can become victims of the very process that they devote their lives to.

Get unstuck from addiction to work!

First, recognize that work addiction exists in your life. You probably had a nagging idea in the back of your brain about your work habits, but it bothered you so you buried it. But then your health started suffering and you didn't take care of yourself because you were working so hard. Now, you feel incredibly tired all the time. Sometimes, you feel really depressed. You definitely aren't happy about your life. An overview of your life can help lift you out of a rut.

Start with yourself first. Change your thinking patterns to design a more stress-free work environment. Even if you're in a high octane, deadline-oriented job, you can make creative changes to give yourself more control over your work load and your time.

Put in new concepts .....

• Make a conscious effort to slow down. Stop and smell a rose or two, or three. Learn to say no when you already have too much on your plate.

• Unless it's an emergency, don't take work home with you. It is important to create time to recharge and nourish yourself physically, mentally, emotionally and spiritually. The quickest path to burnout is to be constantly working or thinking about work. I was surprised to find that I actually thought more clearly and creatively away from work.

• Use relaxation techniques, like yoga, meditation, or a daily walk. Take a tonic, restoring herbal compound like Crystal Star RELAX CAPS™ (with *ashwagandha, black cohosh rt., scullcap, kava kava, black haw, hops, valerian, Eur. mistletoe, wood betony, lobelia, oatstraw).*

• Strengthen family ties. At the end of the day, family is what counts most. Start by celebrating a family tradition or anniversary.

• Cultivate relationships you have in the workplace. New studies link work satisfaction with meaningful interpersonal relationships. Rekindle friendships you let go because of work. Make some new friends. Friends are godsends. They'll expand your interests outside of work.

• Are you organized? Organizing helps de-stress your life. Organization can give you more control, more time and help create a more balanced feeling.

• Develop a hobby or creative outlet you've always wanted to try.

• Improve your diet and get more rest. Live one day at a time.

Is Arthritis A Stress Disease?

The link between stress and arthritis might surprise you.

Arthritis is still the most crippling disease in America. It affects one in seven — about 40 million of us. As we age, the statistics get worse. Eighty percent of people in the U.S. over 50 suffer from arthritis! When you add to that number the people who suffer from arthritis-like diseases, like gout, bursitis, tendonitis, lupus and rheumatoid arthritis, the figure becomes staggering. Arthritis costs the U.S. economy $65 billion in medical care and lost wages *every year*. Most arthritis victims turn to over-the-counter pain killers or powerful prescription drugs for relief. But the downsides to drug therapy are many. Side effects are serious and warning lists are getting longer and longer.

Americans take over 85 million aspirin alone every single day.

For many people, aspirin is part of their daily life. We don't even think of it as a drug. But it is, and like most drugs, even aspirin can hurt your body if used to excess. Aggravating tinnitus (ringing in the ears) and gastrointestinal problems are early signs of aspirin overdose in the body. Later symptoms are more severe. Long term aspirin users are at higher risk for gastric bleeding. The John Hopkins Medical Letter reports that even buffered or enteric coated aspirin is just as likely as regular aspirin to cause gastric bleeding.

Other NSAIDs (non-steroidal anti-inflammatory drugs) like ibuprofen (Advil), and naproxen sodium (Aleve) are equally popular for arthritis pain. For many people, short term, they do reduce crippling arthritis pain. Americans spend a whopping $2.5 billion on NSAIDs each year. But overloading on them can destroy your health. NSAIDs stress your liver and kidneys, cause water retention and are also, like aspirin, linked to serious gastrointestinal problems and bleeding. One-fifth of all adverse drug reactions reported to the FDA are caused by NSAIDs. In 1996, *The Journal of the American Pharmaceutical Association* stated, "Data from studies conducted over the last few years indicates that low dose (60-300mg per day) aspirin and over the counter NSAIDs are associated with significant risk of GI bleeding and upper GI hemorrhage."

More eye opening news: The latest statistics show NSAIDs send 76,000 people to the hospital and kill 7,600 people annually in the U.S. A 1989 study reported in *Lancet* finds NSAIDs actually accelerate joint deterioration!

There's More Bad News on Arthritis Drugs...

Alcohol and arthritis drugs can be a deadly mix. Just a few alcoholic drinks mixed with acetaminophen (as in Tylenol- a pain killer, not an NSAID) can cause liver damage. Several cases of sudden liver failure have already been reported.

Steroid arthritis drugs prescribed for acute flare-ups or serious rheumatoid arthritis cause liver toxicity and eye disorders and may lead to serious diseases like heart disease, diabetes and osteoporosis. Cortisone prescribed for arthritis depresses immunity and can weaken the bones by depleting calcium!

The controversy has led to a new generation of drugs designed to target the pain, but not cause health complications. New "super aspirins" called COX-2 Inhibitors, are being welcomed with open arms by medical professionals and arthritis sufferers. COX-2 Inhibitors work by blocking the enzyme in the body that triggers pain, without blocking the enzyme (COX-1) that protects the stomach. The first COX-2 Inhibitor, Celebrex, was FDA approved in December 1998.

Although the new COX-2 inhibitors are a monumental step towards relieving arthritis symptoms without harming the patient, I advise caution.

The claim: COX-2 inhibitors selectively control inflammation without disrupting body function. The reality: Enzymes are elemental for all body processes. Tampering with enzyms for any length of time has unknown, potentially devastating health effects. Celebrex has caused GI problems in some patients and is linked to a host of side effects. Water retention, headache, indigestion, upper respiratory infection, diarrhea, sinus inflammation, stomach ache and nausea have all been reported. Pregnant women, people with high blood pressure, heart failure, stomach ulcers or or allergies to NSAIDs should avoid Celebrex because of increased health complications.

I don't believe drugs (even the new ones) are the answer for arthritis. Natural arthritis solutions are still your best choice. Here's why:

Arthritis causes are rooted in immune response (highly individual) as well as wear-and-tear effects. Arthritis is caused by a body out of balance.

Arthritis isn't a simple disease. It involves inflammation of the joints, usually accompanied by changes in joint structure. But that's only part of the story. It affects not only the bones and joints, but also the blood vessels (Reynaud's disease), kidneys, skin (psoriasis), eyes and brain. Blood toxicity, poor digestion (usually an overload of heavy meats, rich cheeses and chemicalized foods) are almost always involved.

Emotional stress frequently hastens the onset of arthritis. Stress chemicals (called catecholamines) produce free radicals that ignite the fires of arthritis. Transforming stress into energy is a potent way to erase arthritis symptoms.

Still, arthritis treatment is a place where traditional and natural medicine can come together for the good of the patient. While drugs are a temporary patch for the pain, natural therapies, based in lifestyle and diet changes, work because they address the long term causes of arthritis, not just the symptoms. Anti-arthritic herbs and target supplements not only reduce pain, they also rebalance your body chemistry, rebuild damaged joint structure and improve flexibility. Even doctors now routinely recommend more natural therapies to reduce pain and inflammation without side effects.

Almost everyone over age 50 has signs of arthritis! Is your body showing early signs?
—joint pain or crackling, especially if it develops on one side of the body
—joint deformity or enlargement, usually starting in the knuckles or neck
—morning stiffness during damp weather is an early sign of osteoarthritis
—digestive problems like colitis and food allergies
Long standing lung or bronchial congestion and anemia are signs that your body is congested and out of balance, a favorable environment for arthritis. If this sounds like you, a short arthritis cleanse is a good choice. See page 70.

Is there a difference between osteoarthritis and rheumatoid arthritis?

Rheumatoid arthritis (RA) is an autoimmune condition affecting over 6 million Americans, the vast majority of them women. RA results from an immune system out of control. In RA, your immune system doesn't recognize the difference between itself and an invader. It attacks your own body tissues in the same way it attacks disease-causing bacteria. Symptom onset is quite rapid and the pain and inflammation can cripple. Joints become painfully deformed and organ systems can suffer in late stage RA.

But there is hope. Studies from the University of Denmark reveal ginger is highly effective for pain relief for even serious rheumatoid arthritis. Seventy-four percent of patients report significant pain relief. Add more ginger to your diet. Pickled ginger that comes with sushi, crystallized ginger and grated ginger root are all good choices. Ginger capsules and extracts are widely available at health food stores. To super boost ginger's healing benefits, have a green drink like Crystal Star ENERGY GREEN™ or Nutricology PRO-GREENS WITH FLAX OIL daily to alkalize your body chemistry and release toxins related to RA inflammation.

Rheumatoid arthritis is unique in its close ties to emotional health. Emotional stress frequently brings onset of the disease. Emotional resentments and compulsive behavior traits aggravate RA. Most sufferers have a marked inability to relax (relaxation techniques are essential to healing). Many have a negative attitude toward life that locks up the body's healing ability.

I highly recommend this calming technique for mental stress linked to flare-ups:
—If your mind is racing and you're feeling anxious, shift your focus. Make a sincere effort to turn your attention to your breathing. It's the simplest form of concentrative meditation, the connection between the breath and one's state of mind, a basic principle of yoga relaxation.
—Consciously take slow, deep regular breaths...feel each breath.... for at least one minute.
—Call on your mind-body connection to enhance the calming effect. Recall a pleasant past experience. Remember the good things and people you have in your life. Re-focusing your thoughts to positive feeling helps to neutralize stress reactions linked to arthritis flare-ups.

Natural Solutions For Stress-Related Arthritis

Permanent arthritis healing requires a program not a pill! A comprehensive nutritional and lifestyle approach guarantees much better results. In fact, diet improvement to normalize body chemistry is the single most beneficial thing you can do to control arthritis. Targeted nutrients and herbal therapies also show remarkable success for solving the arthritis problem. I have personally seen notable reduction of swelling, and deformity even in long-standing cases.

Note: *There are up to 100 diseases like rheumatism, bursitis and gout that affect the joints. The program in this book is ideally suited for osteoarthritis, but anyone with a joint disorder can benefit from it.*

Here is my Anti-Arthritis Diet Program:

1: **Eliminate arthritis stressor foods:**
   —fatty meats and dairy foods (animal fats increase the production of inflammatory
      prostaglandins that make your joints hot and red)
   —wheat pastries high in sugar and fat (acid-forming)
   —nightshade foods like peppers, eggplant, tomatoes and potatoes
   —highly salted, spiced foods, caffeine, chocolate, colas and sodas leach out minerals
   —meats like bacon, hot dogs or lunch meats. They carry chemicals that cause joint
      inflammation and degeneration in sensitive people.

2: **Add antioxidant foods.** Free radical damage to cells and tissues is the basis for arthritic aches and pains. Include antioxidants often, from foods like yellow, orange and green vegetables, wheat germ, green tea and citrus fruits to reduce free radical damage and support strong adrenals and balanced hormones (critical for menopausal women).

- Biotec CELL GUARD
- CoQ$_{10}$ 60mg 3x daily
- Grapeseed or white pine PCOs 50mg. 3x daily significantly reduce joint inflammation
- Ester C 500mg with bioflavs for collagen synthesis
- Enzymatic Therapy GRAPE SEED PHYTOSOME 100

3: Use green food therapy. Deep gr eens like alfalfa or barley grass are anti-inflammatory, enzyme rich and a good source of chlorophyll to purify the blood and digestive tract. Many people report significant relief just from drinking green barley juice or taking alfalfa tabs daily.
- Transitions EASY GREENS
- Etherium Technology LIFESOURCE
- NutriCology PRO-GREENS or QUERCETIN 300
- Body Ecology VITALITY SUPERGREEN
- Transformation SUPER CELLZYME caps
- Vibrant Health GREEN VIBRANCE

4: Get more essential fatty acids. EFAs reduce the inflammatory response. Omega-3 rich seafoods like salmon and tuna should be a regular part of your anti-arthritis diet. Sea vegetables like nori, dulse, sea palm and wakame are another healthy option with plenty of EFAs. Sea plants contain all the necessary elements for life, many of which are depleted in the earth's soil. Our bodies use their rich source of nutrients for body structure building blocks.

Omega-3 flax oil provides the essential fatty acids the body needs to protect cell membranes from inflammatory prostaglandins (tissue like hormones that make your joints hot and red). Whole grains, nuts, seeds and beans are also good sources of protein and essential fatty acids.

5: Add enzymes. Extensive research in large controlled studies (over 1000 patients) using supplemental enzymes to treat arthritis and rheumatism, show between 76% to 96% of the patients considerably improved. The enzymes reduced stiffness and joint swelling, increased ability to bend, and slowed down or completely halted the deterioration of the joints.

Enzymes with meals mean better digestion and assimilation of critical nutrients.

—Herbal Products and Development POWER PLUS ENZYMES. They may be use long term and work well for both men and women.

—Transformation Enzyme REPAIRZYME - contains powerful antioxidants, anti-inflammatory agents, enzymes which repair muscle, tissue and skeletal structure.

—Transformation Enzyme PURE-ZYME (protease) carries protein-bound calcium; a protease deficiency lays the foundation for arthritis, osteoporosis and calcium-deficient diseases.

—Bitters herbs provide enzymes and stimulate bile production: CRYSTAL STAR BITTERS & LEMON CLEANSE™ Extract (with *Oregon grape rt., gentian, cardamom, lemon peel, senna, dandelion rt. and leaf, peppermint, honey.*)

6: Add cultured foods for probiotics. It doesn't matter how good your diet is if your body can't use it. If you're taking steroid anti-inflammatory drugs for your arthritis symptoms they may have an adverse effect on your body's ability to use nourishment. Your body ecology must maintain a balance of bacteria to protect immune function. If unfriendly bacteria get the upper hand in the balance, the door opens to infections and allergy reactions. Probiotic organisms prevent disease, even treat infections by restoring microorganism balance in the intestinal tract.

I see probiotic supplements as a health insurance policy today. You can add them through foods such as yogurt and kefir, or as supplements. Lactobacillus acidophilus, (which attaches in the small intestine), bifidobacterius (which attaches in the large intestine) and lactobacillus bulgaricus (three protective strains of flora), produce hydrogen peroxide, a byproduct that helps maintain protective microbial balance and protects against pathogens.

Probiotics not only boost friendly intestinal flora and help your enzyme activity, they also play a key role in bone and joint health (and in preventing osteoporosis). Bone loss is an unfortunate result of a lack of friendly microorganisms in the gastrointestinal tract. Vitamin K, a vital building block to healthy bones, is a byproduct of lactobacilli. I recommend Transformation Enzyme PLANTADOPHILUS for women, and Professional Nutrition DOCTOR-DOPHILUS + FOS for men.

7: **Add a Potassium Essence Broth**. If you're taking steroid drugs that leach potassium, zinc and vitamin C, have a potassium broth once a day for energy, minerals and electrolytes.

For a 2 day supply: Cover with water in a soup pot 4 CARROTS, 3 STALKS CELERY, $\frac{1}{2}$ BUNCH PARSLEY, 2 POTATOES with skins, $\frac{1}{2}$ HEAD CABBAGE, 1 ONION, and $\frac{1}{2}$ BUNCH BROCCOLI.

Simmer covered 30 minutes. Strain and discard solids. Add 2 teasp. Bragg's LIQUID AMINOS or 1 tsp. MISO.

8: **Water may be the most important nutrient in your arthritis diet.** At the cellular level, lack of water (dehydration) slows down all cell processes. Arthritis is a disease linked to dehydration. One of the nutrients used for arthritis is chondroitin sulfate. Chondroitin sulfate is the molecule in cartilage that attracts and holds water. Since healthy joints are 85-90% water, and since cartilage doesn't have its own blood supply, chondroitin sulfate aids the "molecular sponge" that provides nourishment, waste removal and lubrication in healthy joints.

Fluid retention helps restore healthy cartilage and so often relieves osteoarthritic symptoms. Drink 8 to 10 8-oz glasses of water everyday. Limit your use of alcoholic beverages since they are especially dehydrating.

I recommend the day by day cleansing regimen on the following page to get arthritis out of your life.

Small, subtle dietary changes are not successful in reversing arthritic conditions. Vigorous diet therapy is necessary. For permanent results, the diet must be changed to non-mucous and non-sediment-forming foods. The following brief diet programs for arthritis may be used for several weeks to help detoxify the body and flush out inorganic mineral deposits.
Note: Drink 6 to 8 glasses of bottled mineral water daily to keep inorganic wastes releasing quickly from the body.

Begin your arthritis control program with a cleansing diet for 2 to 3 days.

On rising: take a glass of lemon juice and water; or a glass of fresh grapefruit juice. (Acidic foods like citrus fruits generate the production of enzymes that help alkalize the body.)

Breakfast: take a glass of potassium broth or essence; or a glass of carrot/ beet/cucumber juice.

Mid-morning: have apple or black cherry juice; or a green drink, such as Sun Chlorella, Green Foods Green Essence, or Crystal Star Energy Green™ Drink.

Lunch: have miso soup with sea veggies snipped on top, and a glass of fresh carrot juice.

Mid-afternoon: have another green drink, or Crystal Star Green Tea Cleanser™; or an herb tea like alfalfa/mint, or Crystal Star Cleansing & Purifying™ Tea.

Dinner: have a glass of cranberry/apple, or papaya juice, or another glass of black cherry juice.

Before bed: take a glass of celery juice, some Rejuvenative Foods Vegi-Delite; or miso soup.

Keep arthritis away with a fresh foods diet for 3 to 4 weeks.

On rising: take a glass of lemon juice and water, or grapefruit juice; or a glass of apple cider vinegar in water with honey.

Breakfast: have a glass of cranberry, grape or papaya juice, or Crystal Star Biofla-vonoid, Fiber & C Support™ Drink; and fresh fruits like cherries, bananas, oranges and strawber-ries; and take 2 tsp. daily of the following mix. Two TBS. each: sunflower seeds, lecithin gran-ules, brewer's yeast, wheat germ. Mix into yogurt, sprinkle on fresh fruit or greens.

Mid-morning: take a glass of potassium drink; or a tea such as Crystal Star Green Tea Cleanser™, or Green Foods Beta Carrot with 1 tsp. Bragg's Liquid Aminos added.

Lunch: have a large dark green leafy salad with lemon/flax oil dressing; and/or a hot veggie broth or onion soup; and/or some marinated tofu or tempeh in tamari sauce.

Mid-afternoon: have a cup of miso soup with sea veggies snipped on top; or a green drink, alfalfa/mint tea, or Crystal Star Cleansing & Purifying™ Tea.

Dinner: have a Chinese greens salad with sesame or poppy seed dressing made with flax oil; or a large dinner salad with soy cheese, nuts, tamari dressing, and a cup of black bean or miso soup; or some steamed vegetables and brown rice for absorbable B vitamins.

Before bed: have a cranberry or apple juice, or black cherry juice; some Rejuvenative Foods Vegi-Delite or miso extract broth; and/or celery juice.

As the body starts to rebuild, supplements may be added to speed the process along.

—Ascorbate Vitamin C powder and bioflavonoids in juice ($1/_4$ teasp. four times daily) for interstitial tissue and collagen development.

—Add Rainbow Light Advanced Enzyme System and alfalfa tabs 10 daily to alkalize the system.

—Quercetin with bromelain 500mg daily to aid release of inorganic mineral deposits.

—DLPA 750 - 1000mg daily for pain relief.

—Capsaicin creme as needed to help joint pain, flexibility and circulation.

Herbal nutrients are some of my favorite healers for arthritis.

• Bioflavonoids restore structural support and prevent collagen from being destroyed by chronic arthritis inflammation. Bioflavonoids, vitamin C and fiber speed arthritic waste removal. Consider Crystal Star Bioflavonoid, Fiber & Vit. C Support™, a citrus and herb drink mix.

• Many herbs can relieve inflammation, reduce pain, and dissolve inorganic sediment trapped in joints. Devil's claw is a superior choice for herbal treatment because it can do all three. Scientific studies validate its effectiveness. Use it with other anti-inflammatory herbs like yucca and black cohosh that boost its benefits. Crystal Star Ar-Ease™ Caps (with *yucca, alfalfa sd., devil's claw rt., guggul, buckthorn, dandelion, bilberry, parsley, burdock, black cohosh, rose hips extract, slippery elm, St. John's wort, yarrow, hydrangea, licorice, hawthorn, turmeric, ligusticum, poria*) and Gaia Herbs Devil's Claw/Chaparral Supreme are both designed for healthy joints.

Medical focus of diagnosis has been on organic mineral depletion (especially calcium) as a cause of arthritis. Hormone imbalance and adrenal exhaustion are also critical to repair, especially for menopausal women.

• Boost adrenal health. Exhausted adrenals from chronic stress are at the root of many women's problems including menopausal arthritis. Consider an adrenal boosting herbal formula like Crystal Star Adr-Active™ (with *licorice, sarsaparilla, bladderwrack, uva ursi, Irish moss, ginger, astragalus, capsicum, rose hips extract*). I formulated it for my own wiped out adrenals over 20 years ago and it's still one of the top compounds in the Crystal Star line. Other adrenal therapy: YS Royal Jelly/Ginseng; Enzymatic Therapy Adrenal Cortex Complex; American Biologics Sub-Adrene.

• *Burdock root* is an excellent arthritis remedy because it bolsters the immune system (usually depressed in arthritis), reduces joint swelling and balances hormones. Simmer 1-2 tsp. of the dried root in a cup of water for 15 minutes. Take 3 times a week for the best results.

Super supplements can wipe out arthritis symptoms.

• European studies on chrondroitin sulfate (CSA), a supplement derived from the shells of soft-shelled crabs, show highly effective relief for arthritic pain. CSA supplements attract water to joints and improve the elasticity and fluidity of joint movement. Glucosamine sulfate (GS), an amino acid complex, prompts the production of connective tissue in order to build new cartilage which provides lubrication and cushioning for body joints. Tests have even found it be superior to ibuprofen in terms of pain relief! Using a cartilage protective product with *both supplements* provides maximum benefits with no reported toxic side effects. We've tested Country Life Glucosamine Complex, Allergy Research Matrix and Enzymatic Therapy Gs-Complex for effectiveness.

Anti-inflammatories:

• MSM (methylsulfonylmethane) is a crystalline carrier of sulfur (low sulphur usually means inflammation), a mineral for building body tissue especially skin, hair, nails and joints. MSM supports cell flow-through, a benefit that allows harmful substances, like lactic acid and toxins, to flow out while permitting nutrients to flow in. This prevents a pressure buildup in the cells which contributes to inflammation in the joints. A recent study in the Journal of Anti-Aging Medicine, showed that 80% of patients treated with MSM experienced significant pain relief after six weeks. 750 to 1000 mg. ($^1/_4$ to $^1/_2$ teasp.) a day is a therapeutic dose.
Note: MSM is synergistic with vitamin C and it requires the trace element, molybdenum to metabolize. Look for products at health food stores which contain all three nutrients.

• Protease (an enzyme that digests protein), accelerates the anti-inflammatory process. It helps decrease pain, swelling, redness, heat, and loss of function. Transformation PUREZYME fights inflammation and boosts the immune system.

Other effective anti-inflammatories for arthritis:
—DLPA 750mg daily
—Crystal Star ANTI-FLAM™ CAPS (with *white willow, St. John's wort, echinacea angustifolia and purpurea rt., white pine, gotu kola, red clover, devil's claw, alfalfa, burdock, dandelion, chamomile, uva ursi, ginger, bromelain 22mg*).
—Quercetin with bromelain 1000mg daily
—Zinc for inflammation control, and tissue regeneration. I like herbal sources best so you don't take too much. Crystal Star ZINC SOURCE™ EXTRACT (with *echinacea, spirulina, gotu kola, peppermint, bilberry, yellow dock, alfalfa, barley grass, propolis, peppermint*) is effective.
—Allergy Research CURCUMIN/BROMELAIN
—Prevail MOBILE

• Use chlorophyll sources to help stimulate cortisone.
—Solaray ALFA-JUICE caps
—Crystal Star ENERGY GREEN™ DRINK
—NutriCology PRO-GREENS WITH FLAX OIL
—Wakunaga KYO-GREEN
—Body Ecology VITALITY SUPERGREEN

Do topical pain relievers work for arthritis?

The most innovative products incorporate glucosamine sulfate and hormone stimulants like pregnenolone into topical creams. Many people experience significant pain reduction. I've talked to Wakunaga, one of the new product developers, and their early reports look very good. Their FREEDOM ARTHRITIS RELIEF CREAM combines glucosamine sulfate, emu oil and pregnenolone.

• Popular Capsaicin creams use an extract of cayenne pepper to stimulate circulation and reduce arthritis inflammation. U.S. tests find it is effective for more than 80% of arthritis swelling. Nature's Way CAYENNE HERBAL PAIN RELIEVING OINTMENT contains .25% Capsaicin.

Bodywork therapies are essential for overcoming arthritis.

Don't quit on exercise! Light exercise is a key to improving joint flexibility and makes tasks like walking, climbing stairs and getting in and out of cars easier if you have arthritis. A 1997 study in *Journal of the American Medical Association* finds that patients with osteoarthritis improve after an aerobic or resistance training exercise program. Exercise helps release the stress and anger and frees up energy blocks involved in arthritis, too. Play it safe. Joint injuries caused by "extreme sports" may result in arthritis-like aches for years to come.

• Massage therapy helps if pain is making you depressed. The chronic pain of arthritis can lead to depression, stress and hopelessness, especially in the elderly. I recommend massage therapy, a natural pain killer and stress reducer that boosts brain serotonin, a neurotransmitter low in depressed people. Actual anti-depressant effects of a half hour massage last from 3 to 36 hours!

You can sweat out arthritis pain!

An arthritis sweat is an effective, ancient technique to help eliminate offending crystalline deposits in connective tissue and relieve stiffness. A surprising amount of arthritis-aggravating material can be eliminated via the skin. A sweat is also a good way to start an arthritis cleanse (page 70). Results increase when sweating herbs like elder flowers, peppermint or yarrow are taken in a hot tea along with the bath.
Note: If you have a weak heart or hypertension, consult a health professional before trying an arthritis sweat bath.

Here's how to take the bath:
Use about 3 pounds of Epsom salts (or as directed for Dead Sea salts). Run hot bath water and add the salts. Let cool enough to get in. Try to stay in the bath for 15 to 20 minutes. Rub affected joints with a stiff brush in the water for 5 to 10 minutes. On emerging, do not dry yourself. Instead, wrap up immediately in a clean sheet and go straight to bed, covering yourself with several blankets. The osmotic pressure of the salt solution absorbed by the sheet will draw off heavy perspiration (protect your mattress with a sheet of plastic). The following morning the sheet will be stained with yellowish brown material excreted from your skin. Continue treatment once every two weeks until the sheet is no longer stained, a sign that your body is cleansed. Drink plenty of water throughout the procedure to prevent dehydration and loss of body salts. Arthritis improvement after an Epsom salt bath experience is notable.

Chart your own arthritis improvement.

Here are some of the benefits most people notice as their bodies begin to respond to diet changes and stress reducing techniques:

1: Reduced inflammation and swelling, usually noticed early in your program.
2: Stiffness subsides, within 2 to 3 weeks. Regenerating flexibility may take
   longer — several months as cartilage and connective tissue rebuild.
3: Better skin tone, digestive health and bowel regularity.
4: Eye and skin moisture improves because mucous membrane health improves.
5: Immune response improves — you'll experience fewer colds and flu.

Are You In An Energy Crunch?

Do you just plain need more energy? Even when you aren't under stress?

Modern life is plagued with a human energy shortfall. Like drilling for oil in the ground, we dig deeper for more energy reserves, and more often than not come up dry. Americans live hurried, high pressure lives. Our society and culture are moving at such a fast pace that there are precious few tried and true ways to cling to, or knowledge to fall back on. We're moving fast, but noise and pollution are moving faster. We're stripping our bodies and brains of oxygen and nutrients that provide us with fuel for work and productivity. Our daily rush takes its toll in blood pressure, hormone, heart and breathing changes. These changes make you feel really tired and burned out for no apparent reason. Even if you lead a "normal" life without obvious stress, life in the nineties is no walk in the park.

I don't know anyone who doesn't want to increase energy. How about you? Perhaps you want to take on an extra job to meet financial obligations. Maybe you want to start an exercise program. There's a night school course you always wanted to take (or teach). You'd like to go on an active vacation, like a rainforest eco-tour or an archaeology dig or a sailboat cruise. You'd definitely like to spend some active time with your kids. There's so much you want to do..... but you're so TIRED all the time.

How do we make up this depletion of our energy reserves?

We might take in more food for fuel; but even eating more of the right foods is not always the best choice for bosting our energy and, certainly, maintaining a healthy weight. And it's hard to get readily available tissue energy from most foods, since nutrients necessarily follow slow, circuitous routes through the digestive system.

We might go for chemical stimulants — like drugs or caffeine. But we know they're really a dead end for energy and oxygen needs. After a short period of stimulation, these substances constrict rather than open up blood flow, especially to the brain. Most are harmful to the liver and other vital organs, and in the end most are addictive.

I think you need to start at the top...

Boosting Your Mental Energy

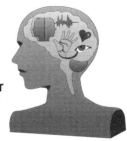

Your brain controls your entire body. The brain may be only 2% of your body weight, but it uses over 20% of your total energy supply and 25% of your total oxygen intake. Your brain is also your primary health mainte-nance organ and the seat of energy production.

The brain is incredibly sensitive. Drugs and stimulants like alcohol, caffeine and tobacco accelerate its activity for a short time, but then actually depress its function. Food and environ-mental toxins play a role in mental decline as well. Fluoride, aspartame (Nutrasweet), alumi-num, MSG, are all substances that have been implicated in the destruction of brain cells. A diet high in refined sugar actually decreases the amount of blood sugar available to the brain.

Stress impacts your brain. If too much of the stress hormone (cortisol) is produced in the brain, mental function declines.

Your brain needs the right nutrients to think... to be creative, to solve problems, to remember things. New clinical trials show that your brain's neurotransmitter levels can be significantly increased by a single nutritious meal!

Your brain holds about ten *billion* neurons which must be constantly supplied with glucose, oxygen, vitamins, minerals, amino acids and fatty acids by the bloodstream. In fact, our brain cells consume 50% of our blood glucose (sugar), five times more glucose than other cells in the body, because its neurons have such complex, fuel demanding communication duties. Your brain is almost totally dependent on you and the nutrition you give it, for high quality fuel. Other organs aren't so exposed; they can use fats and starches as well as glucose for energy.

Brain nutrients affect brain performance — positively and rapidly! Consistent, brain neurotransmitter replenishment can straighten out even grave mental, emotional and coordination problems. The brain has a large appetite. Examples of brain foods that can supply these nutrients include: sea foods and sea vegetables of all kinds, sprouts, fertile eggs, wheat germ, unsaturated vegetable oils, brown rice, spinach, tofu, apples, oranges, canteloupe, grapefruit, wheat germ and beans. Cold water fish are one of the best brain foods because they are primarily essential fatty acids and water.

The Gut-Brain Connection: Brain neurons are highly dependent on your digestive system to take in the nutrients it needs. Your brain needs your colon to be working well, too. The brain uses nutrients so quickly, that toxins from the colon and digestive tract can pass rapidly to brain cells. Researchers have found links between toxins like ammonia in the GI tract, and neurological diseases like schizophrenia and autism.

The Enzyme-Brain Connection: Enzymes are the ignition sparks for the assimilation and use of every nutrient we take in. Enzymes are inhibited by stress responses. Focus on fresh plant foods for plenty of dietary enzymes. They are essential in producing neurotransmitters like serotonin for stress-energy balance. If you can't make enzymes, take them. Consider Transformation CALMZYME ENZYMES to feed and fortify the nervous system against stress reactions.

Antioxidants nourish and protect your brain against stress.

New stress tests convince many scientists that senile dementia and other nerve damage diseases have their origins in free radical damage that can be helped by antioxidants.

Which antioxidants are the best for the brain? Besides well-known antioxidants like Vitamin C, Vitamin E, selenium, carotenes and CoQ-10, herbal antioxidants are some of the most important protectors against free radical damage to the brain and nerves.

Three herbs are especially effective for mental acuity.

Rosemary, known since ancient times as a memory enhancer (remember the line in Shakespeare's HAMLET where Ophelia offers Hamlet some *rosemary* for remembrance?), is an adrenal cortex stimulant and a brain tonic. *Rosemary* has a particularly potent antioxidant called rosmarinic acid which fights free radical damage to brain cells. It also contains a number of compounds that prevent the breakdown of acetylcholine, a brain chemical linked to memory. The most rapid way to use rosemary is to use a fresh sprig or two (high in oils) steeped in a tea for ten minutes, or in wine for several hours. Take small sips of either... a little goes a long way.

Ginkgo biloba, a plant used for thousands of years to improve mental acuity, dilates the vascular system and inhibits platelet aggregation (cell clumping) to promote free blood flow to the brain. Decreased blood flow to the brain is linked to age-related brain disorders like Alzheimer's. *Ginkgo* has been called a perfect brain food, because it scavenges superoxide and peroxyl radicals that damage brain cells, and also increases glucose uptake for brain food. *Ginkgo* treats specific age-related cerebral insuffiency symptoms: absentmindedness, anxiety, confusion, decreased physical performance, depression, difficult concentration, poor long-term and short-term memory, dizziness, low energy and ringing in the ears. It's most effective in liquid or powdered extract form, at a dose of 40mg 3 times a day. The *ginkgo* tree is incredibly resilient; a solitary *ginkgo biloba* survived the Hiroshima nuclear blast and still stands today.

Gotu Kola, a brain and nerve rejuvenating tonic, improves learning, poor concentration and memory. As with *ginkgo*, *gotu kola* is an ancient Asian-Indian longevity herb. Legends say that *gotu kola* was first used by natives of Ceylon for better memory when it was noticed that their elephants, noted for their long lives and superb memories, fed on the herb. Modern day people of the Indian sub-continent eat *gotu kola* in their salads and take it as a hot drink.

Gotu kola is a specific adaptogenic herb for conquering the effects of stress and fatigue. Like *ginkgo*, *gotu kola* improves circulation to the brain and strengthens arteries and veins. Even more than *ginkgo*, it's nerve repair and restorative ability makes *gotu kola* useful for anxiety-stress reactions. I find it highly useful for promoting mental alertness without caffeine-like side effects. It is effective as a tea for children with hyperactive attention deficit disorder.

Crystal Star MENTAL CLARITY™ CAPS (with *American ginseng rt. (panax), gotu kola, fo-ti, kelp, ginkgo biloba, Siberian ginseng, rosemary, schizandra, choline, prickly ash bk., capsicum, and l-glutamine)*, is a frequent choice of students and professional people who need concentrated mental acuity. The high grade *ginsengs* and antioxidants can usually be felt right away.

But your brain needs more.

Minerals provide significant bio-neuro-transmission — the key to your body. Electrolytic potassium, zinc and trace minerals chromium, num are all important for brain health. these ingredients. In fact, minerals are day they're far more likely to be defi-amino acids or enzymes, especially in

chemical ingredients for brain your brain's communication with magnesium, calcium, iodine, iron, boron, manganese and molybde-Mineral-rich herbs are providers of critical to brain function; yet to-cient in the diet than vitamins, diets that lack whole foods.

Your brain depends on the nutrients choline, tyrosine and tryptophan to synthesize neurotransmitters. If you're noticing slow or poor memory, or less mental sharpness than you're used to, consider boosting your brain's levels of these nutrients.

• Choline, a member of the B-complex family, increases brain choline and acetylocholine levels linked to memory activity. Choline can enhance memory and revitalize your brain so that you feel energetic all over. Studies at M.I.T. show that choline is effective in treating manic-depressive mental illness, Alzheimer's and tardive dyskinesia. Choline is one of the few nutrients that is able to penetrate the blood-brain barrier, so it passes directly into the brain cells. Food sources of choline include: egg yolks, meat, and fish. Lecithin is a good supplement source of choline from soybeans or sunflower seeds.

• Tyrosine, an amino acid, increases the production of dopamine and norepinephrine, neurotransmitters that buffer the effects of stress on your glands and nerves. Dopamine and norepinephrine also regulate blood pressure, heart rate, muscle tone, brain metabolism and nervous system function. Tyrosine improves mental alertness and quick response, eases anxiety and helps to relieve tension. It also protects your brain from the shock of extreme stress. Food sources include: whole grains, soybeans, legumes, dairy products, fish and meat. If you decide to take it as a supplement, about 500mg daily is a normal dose.

• Tryptophan, an amino acid, influences the neurotransmitter serotonin, which makes you more relaxed. Tryptophan helps your thinking to stay clearer and eases other mental and physical effects of stress. Food sources include: brown rice, corn, legumes and most dairy foods.

And don't forget.....
• B vitamins are essential in synthesizing neurotransmitters, and in forming the myelin sheath, a shield substance that insulates the connections between neurons so they can transmit messages effectively. They're important for maintaining a healthy brain-immune connection, too. Symptoms associated with Alzheimer's, like memory loss, emotional instability and reduced attention span accompany B vitamin deficiencies.

• Calcium and magnesium stabilize and protect brain membranes. Magnesium helps manufacture ATP, energy for the cells and it is essential for the enzymes that produce neurotransmitters. Magnesium even helps prevent migraine headaches. Calcium boosts the potential of nerve and muscle cells so that they can communicate through electrical impulses.

• Superfoods can help your brain. I recommend multi-talented herbal superfoods to insure a full spectrum of essential nutrients necessary for brain health. Here are some choices:
—Etherium Technology LIFESOURCE
—NutriCology PRO-GREENS
—Body Ecology VITALITY SUPERGREEN
—Gaia Herbs GINKGO/GOTU KOLA SUPREME

•Crystal Star MEDITATION TEA™ (with *cardamom, ginger rt., cloves, fennel sd., cinnamon and peppercorns*) promotes brain alpha activity, lifting the mind to greater awareness and focus.

Does ginseng really boost mental energy?

Millions of people have taken tons of *ginseng* for thousands of years to promote health, restore body balance, and increase strength and stamina. I myself have interviewed hundreds of people who took high quality *ginseng* for clearer thinking. Without exception, they felt that both memory and alertness improved, and that they had more energy during the day.

Now scientific studies are confirming *ginseng's* anti-stress, endurance-enhancing effects. While modern tests have focused on memory, concentration, alertness and learning ability in the elderly, it's clear that ginseng is able to raise spirits and improve outlook for a wide range of people.

Ginseng can get you back up to speed after a hard day's night, too, because its adaptogenic, tonic character helps normalize body chemistry. The best formula I know is Crystal Star GINSENG SIX™ SUPER ENERGY CAPS (with *bee pollen, Siberian ginseng, gotu kola, fo ti, Chinese kirin ginseng, prince ginseng, suma, aralia, alfalfa, dong quai and l-glutamine*).

The botanical kingdom offers several other herbs that help bring about improved alertness, stimulate brain activity, and rejuvenate tired brain and memory centers. *Gotu kola, prince ginseng* and *damiana* in the following tea help maintain mental vigor and provide long term brain nourishment. Crystal Star CREATIVI-TEA™ (with *gotu kola, kava kava, prince ginseng rt., damiana, licorice rt., muira puama, juniper bry., cloves, spearmint*).

Mental stress and depression are severe deterrents to good brain function. An anti-stress herbal combination can provide a restorative measure of calm during grief or unidentified lingering depression. Crystal Star DEPRESS-EX™ CAPS (with *St. John's wort, kava kava, American ginseng rt., ashwagandha, gotu kola, scullcap, Siberian ginseng, rosemary, wood betony, fo ti, ginger*) is effective for nervous exhaustion due to emotional trauma or stress.

St. John's wort acts pharmacologically to alter brain chemistry in ways similar to anti-depressant drugs, but without the side effects of those drugs. I find it works far better in a combination like Crystal Star DEPRESS-EX™ EXTRACT (with *scullcap, valerian, rosemary, ashwagandha, St. John's wort, hops flwr., catnip, wood betony, peppermint, celery sd., cinnamon, honey, anise*) with other nervine and adaptogenic (stress handling) herbs.

Exercise brings oxygen to your brain to deal with stress-induced reactions. New studies show that deep breathing and exercise are better than drugs at reducing anxiety. Exercise helps neutralize metabolic by-products of stress, stimulates secretion of naturally tranquilizing endorphins to diffuse stress, and potentiates production of neurotransmitters.

Boredom is the biggest stress for your brain. Challenge your brain to improve it. New experiences, memory stretching games, regular reading and crossword puzzles all activate mental development. Research shows that brain stimulation cultivates new projections from existing nerve cells. Your brain actually physically expands with new knowledge!

Subtle energies - a new answer for mental energy?

The cutting-edge, biochemical field of subtle energies includes all energy interactions that influence our bodies. Based on the premise that before we are a physical body we are an energy field, even low-level changes in magnetic, electric, electromagnetic, acoustic, and gravity can have profound effects on our biology and our psychology. Amazingly, it has been documented that humans are capable of *generating* and controlling subtle, not-yet-measurable energies that influence both physical and mental mechanisms. Many popular complementary therapies involve the flow of these subtle energies. Earth and plant energies are now known to support and strengthen us. Electromagnetic pollution (EMFs) disrupt our harmony with natural energies.

New products are emerging which focus on the relationship of the energy fields that emanate from foods, herbs and minerals, and their effect on human energy fields. Etherium Technology ETHERIUM GOLD is a naturally occurring, unique trace mineral composite with a rare double vortex pattern and a high electrical potential with high standing waves. The vortexes closely resemble the pattern energy creates when it transforms into matter. Richard Gerber, M.D., author of *Vibrational Medicine*, comments, "Physically, ETHERIUM GOLD enhances interconnectivity. Its rare trace elements such as gold, rhodium, and iridium produce a natural biological superconductivity that enhances communication between the nervous system and body tissues." Nearly everyone tested showed a positive benefit from using the COLLOIDAL SILVER, SILICA AND GOLD product. Etherium Technology, Inc. 16004 SW Tualatin Sherwood Rd., Suite 503, Sherwood, OR 97140, 503-625-2880.

Studies using biofeedback and neurofeedback equipment on subjects taking the subtle energies product found an increase in "neurological energy" across all freqency bands. The positive neurological impact provided an environment for the brain to become more balanced and calm after administration of the product. In addition, GSR measurements indicated a decrease in emotional reactivity and greater relaxation.

If you're interested.... the International Society for the Study of Subtle Energies and Energy Medicine (ISSSEEM Publications 303-425-4625) publish a peer-reviewed scientific journal with studies of subtle energies and information systems that interact with the human psyche and physiology.

Breathe energy into your brain

Brain breathing is one of the best ways I know to energize your mind. The brain breathing techniques in this section are very effective. Oxygen is the most vital and essential ingredient for life. Oxygen directly stimulates our brain, our logic and our intelligence. Your brain requires three times more oxygen than the rest of your body. Oxygen is essential to the production of energy and the heart of metabolism. Without oxygen, the energy of the food you eat could not be released to you. One expert, Philip Rice, M.D., a delinquent child specialist, said "Fifty-five percent of the delinquent behavior in children can be attributed to oxygen starvation."

Oxygen starvation is linked to shallow breathing, a lack of exercise and a lack of fresh air. Without a sufficient supply of oxygen, the bloodstream becomes saturated with poisonous carbon dioxide and other toxic wastes. The more deeply you breathe, the greater the delivery of oxygen to the brain and all body cells. Deep brain breathing oxygenates and rejuvenates you to a higher vibration of living. It can step up your physical, mental and spiritual capabilities.

Here is the Paul Bragg *Super Power Brain Breathing* exercise: Repeat 5 times
1: Stand erect with feet slightly apart for balance.
2: Slowly inhale through your nose and mouth and raise your hands overhead — pushing downward with your diaphragm and expanding your chest.
3: Hold your breath to the slow count of 10, and bend forward like you are going to touch your toes. This allows the oxygenated blood to suffuse the pituitary gland and recharge every part of the brain for sharper thinking.
4: After your count and still holding your breath, come back up to the standing position.
5: When you reach the standing position, exhale vigorously while bending forward.
6: Inhale slowly while coming back up.
Note: If it is hard to hold your breath or you feel dizzy, inhale and gradually build up to a full count.

Deep breathing / diaphragmatic breathing calms the nervous system. The center of the diaphragm holds a network of nerves and nerve groups influenced by breathing. The more stimulation from the breath (oxygen), the more *nerve energy* is available for nerve strength and nerve balance and calmness. Your vital organs (liver, intestines, kidneys, gallbladder, spleen and pancreas) thrive on nerve energy. Diaphragmatic breathing boosts blood circulation, massages and exercises your abdominal muscles, heart and chest.

Here is the Paul Bragg *Super Power Breath* exercise: Repeat 5 times
1: Stand erect with feet apart for good balance.
2: Slowly inhale through your nose and mouth and raise your hands overhead — pushing downward with your diaphragm and expanding your chest.
3: Bend forward as if to touch your toes and exhale at the same time through your mouth.
4: Again slowly inhale through your nose and mouth and return to the standing position with hands raised overhead. Draw in air to the full capacity of your lungs.

See Paul & Patricia Bragg's *Super Power Breathing For Super Energy* book for more.

Is your thyroid sluggish?

If your energy is unusually low.... if you've put on a few extra pounds even though your eating habits haven't changed... if you're feeling inexplicably tired... if you're chronically constipated... if you're always cold, even when it's warm outside... if you're depressed for no real reason... you may have an underactive thyroid, and it will affect your energy levels.

Thyroid disease affects an astounding eleven million Americans.

Almost 85% are women, and for most women especially after menopause, the problem is low thyroid (hypothyroidism). The symptoms are so close to those of severe stress reactions that low thyroid is often diagnosed as depression - or ignored as emotional anxiety. Some experts today, think thyroid imbalance of all kinds is an immune disorder, where your body's own immune defenses attack your thyroid. They say poor thyroid function could be accounted for by a mineral-poor diet, environmental pollutants, even certain household or food chemicals. It is known that an above average number of people born since World War II (when many of the chemicals we use today came into our culture) have thyroid disease. Many Americans have benign nodules on their thyroid, not cancerous, but signifying an abnormal thyroid condition.

The thyroid is your body's energy gland. It's a system balancing gland, normalizing metabolic rates, stabilizing energy use and energy production, and regulating hormones, like estrogen and progesterone. The thyroid needs a regular supply of certain minerals, especially potassium and iodine, to produce its wide array of balancers. I believe the naturally-occurring iodine and minerals in herbs and sea plants is the best way to take these minerals in today.

Thyroid support herbs have many advantages. Herbs are at their best as body balancers; they can enhance other organ functions - kidneys, gallbladder and pancreas — as they encourage a lazy thyroid. Crystal Star IODINE THERAPY™ CAPS (with *kelp, alfalfa, dandelion, dulse, spirulina, barley grass, nettle, borage sd., watercress*) have plenty of iodine and potassium for your thyroid along with accompanying minerals to help your body use them best.

Note: Thyroid health is primary to metabolic activity. Many people use thyroid support herbs effectively as part of a weight control program for middle age spread. Crystal Star META-TABS™ (with *Irish moss, kelp, parsley, watercress, sarsaparilla, mullein, lobelia and carrot*).

Is tired blood keeping your energy low?

Is your circulation a sluggish stream instead of a river of life? Your bloodstream provides your body with nutrients and oxygen, and takes away body waste. Red blood cells carry the nutrients, and five major types of white blood cells (vital to immunity) attack invading bacteria, viruses and parasites. Even at rest, almost sixteen pints of blood surges through your veins and arteries and your heart beats an average of 70 times per minute (two and a half billion! heart beats in your lifetime).

Imagine your blood as a pristine high country stream that gathers nutrients as it courses down the hills, and fans out in thousands of tributaries to every part of your body. Just like a mountain stream, everything you put into it changes its character. Adding whole, pure nutrients to the stream brings nourishment. Adding chemicalized foods harms it's clean nature just as a stream flowing through a polluted area picks up pollutants. When a stream is channeled at its source into concrete or pipes, it doesn't get a chance to oxygenate, or pick up cleansing minerals along the way to keep itself healthy. If your red bloodstream doesn't get minerals (especially iron), it becomes congested with toxins and can't effectively carry essential oxygen to remote areas of your body. Lack of adequate oxygen results in fatigue, general weakness, memory loss, and cold, sluggish hands and feet.

• You can target your diet to quickly boost blood stimulating nutrients. Many of my favorite superfoods and herbs can help — *chlorella, spirulina, barley grass, ginseng, wheat grass, sea vegetables (like kelp, dulse, wakame, kombu), suma, ginger, capsisum, astragalus and bee pollen.*

• Protease, an enzyme that digests protein, is a powerful blood purifier. Protease digests unwanted debris in the blood including certain bacteria and viruses. Protease deficient people are usually immune compromised, making them susceptible to bacterial, viral and yeast infections, and a general decrease in immunity. Protease is able to dissolve almost all proteins as long as they are not protected by the inhibiting mechanism components of normal living cells. Bacteria, parasites and fungal forms are protein. Viruses are cell parasites consisting of nucleic acids covered by a protein film.

Fresh plant juices are especially important for protease enzyme deficiency. Inadequate protein digestion leads to hypoglycemia resulting in moodiness, mood swing and irritability. A protease deficiency also sets up an environment for arthritis, osteoporosis and other calcium-deficient diseases. Since protein is needed to carry protein-bound calcium in the blood, the first sign of a protease deficiency is unusual anxiety and insomnia.

Plant protease supplements, like Transformation Purezyme can shore up a protease deficiency.

Note: Poor food combining accounts for an amazing amount of iron deficiency anemia. Get a good Food Combination Chart at your natural foods store, or see the Correct Food Combining Chart in **Healthy Healing** - Tenth Edition by Linda Page.

Tired blood can get an energy boost from herbs.

Mineral-rich herbs offer easily assimilated, non-constipating iron along with other minerals that help in iron uptake. A combination like the one below also stimulates the liver and spleen to produce more hemoglobin and energizing oxygen for both blood and brain. An absorbable, non-constipating iron and trace mineral formula is Crystal Star Iron Source™ Caps (with *beet, yellow dock rt., dulse, dandelion, borage, parsley, rosemary, alfalfa*).

Alterative and cardiovascular tonic herbs stimulate sluggish circulation to counteract fatigue.

• Alterative herbs, like *echinacea, burdock, garlic, red clover, sarsaparilla, goldenseal, nettles and yellow dock*, improve blood composition and help purify and cleanse it. Alterative herbs also stimulate improve blood circulation — to bring energy and vitality back into tired blood.

• Cardiovascular tonic herbs, like *capsicum, ginger, garlic and prickly ash* enhance circulation and normalize blood pressure.

• *Hawthorn herb*, even by itself is a powerful circulatory tonic. It works slowly and steadily to strengthen heart and valve muscles, relax blood vessels and stabilize heart rate. *Hawthorn* is unique in that a feeling of well-being is experienced quite soon after beginning a regular course of the extract. For best results, use an extract made from the whole plant, leaf, berry and flower, not just the berries. Check your extract bottle. Important flavonoids are potent and heavy. You can see them settled at the bottom of the bottle before you shake it to take it.

Are blood sugar imbalances sapping your energy reserves?

Imbalances in how your body uses blood sugar are a common cause of energy loss. Both high blood sugar (diabetes symptoms) and low blood sugar (hypoglycemia symptoms) severely exhaust energy. New research shows that blood sugar imbalance creates a yo-yo malfunction. In fact, almost all diabetics, from latent to full-blown, were once hypoglycemic.

Blood sugar (glucose) is your cellular food. The adrenal glands and the pancreas are your body's key organs for regulating blood sugar levels. The pancreas' job is to release insulin which helps reduce excess sugar in the blood. The adrenals release adrenaline which helps to increase sugar levels in the blood.

Balancing your blood sugar can change your whole outlook on life. Energy levels rise and so does creativity. You become a totally different person because sugar imbalances affect health on all levels - physical, mental, emotional, and spiritual. While everyone with blood sugar irregularities should consult a health care professional, diet improvement and specific herbal formulas can help in energy return.

—Low blood sugar (hypoglycemia) happens when the pancreas oversecretes insulin. Excess insulin results in lowering blood sugar too much. Your body strives to achieve proper glucose/insulin balance but the adrenals are unable to bring blood sugar levels up. This is particularly harmful to your brain, the most sensitive organ to blood sugar levels, because your brain requires glucose as an energy source to think clearly. Almost everyone with hypoglycemia has periods of mental confusion or lapses of memory and inability to concentrate. Small sugar fluctuations include an unusually cold nose and a disturbed sense of well-being. Large fluctuations can cause feelings of depression, anxiety, sudden fatigue, mood swings, hyperactivity in children, even aggressive behavior.

—High blood sugar (diabetes), develops when your body doesn't use the insulin hormone correctly, and your food isn't efficiently converted to energy. Symptoms of high blood sugar include: low energy, excessive urination, hypertension and usually accelerated aging.

You can boost your energy by dealing naturally with hypoglycemia. Your diet is clearly the first place to start. Nutrient deficiencies that cause a drop underneath your blood sugar "floor," always accompany hypoglycemia — especially B-vitamins, minerals like chromium, zinc and vanadium, amino acids like alanine and glycine, and sugar-stabilizing fiber and essential fatty acids from whole grains and vegetables. Hypoglycemia attacks are commonly brought on by overconsumption of sugar, caffeine, alcohol and junk (chemicalized) foods. Avoiding these foods is obviously a major step in correcting hypoglycemia energy loss.

Don't make the mistake of thinking that you can eat sugar to help raise low blood sugar. Sugary foods, especially fast food sweets, even natural sugars like honey, molasses and maple syrup, complicate hypoglycemia. Sugary carbohydrates raise glucose levels in a sugar rush, but as the pancreas overcompensates with too much insulin, blood sugar levels drop too far and too fast. Simply avoiding these foods if you are hypoglycemic is far easier said than done. Sugar cravings for people with low blood sugar are monumental, sometimes at addictive levels.

A consistent program of replacing problematic foods with specific foods that help to stabilize blood sugar swings has a much better chance of success. To raise your energy while you stabilize your blood sugar, concentrate your diet on slow, even-burning fuel, high fiber, complex carbohydrates and plant proteins. Eat small, frequent meals, with plenty of fresh foods to keep sugar levels in balance.

1: Eat potassium-rich foods — oranges, broccoli, bananas, and tomatoes

2: Eat chromium-rich foods — brewer's yeast, mushrooms, whole wheat, seafood, beans

3: Eat high quality protein like soy foods, brown rice, seafood, sea plants at every meal

4: Add cultured foods, such as raw sauerkraut or yogurt for G.I. flora

5: Add sea vegetables as a thyroid tonic to address hypoglycemia's underactive thyroid

6: Have a daily superfood green drink to build a "floor" under a sugar drop: Crystal Star ENERGY GREEN™ DRINK, NutriCology PRO-GREENS with flax seed, Etherium LIFESOURCE. Add 2 teasp. daily of YS ROYAL JELLY with *Siberian ginseng* to a protein or green drink for even better results.

I recommend a diet like this for 2 to 3 months until blood sugar levels are regularly stable.

Effective natural strategies for balancing your blood sugar to boost energy.

•Glandular support herbs help support the health of both the adrenals and the pancreas. Crystal Star SUGAR STRATEGY LOW™ caps and tea (with *licorice rt., dandelion, cedar bry., alfalfa, wild yam rt., gotu kola, spirulina, barley grass, guar gum, horseradish, suma*).

• Adrenal stress tonics for low blood sugar include *gotu kola, licorice and Siberian ginseng.* Transformation ULTRAZYME feeds the endocrine system and contains enzymes and herbs which support the adrenal glands. Crystal Star ADRN-ACTIVE™ (with *licorice rt., sarsaparilla, bladderwrack, uva ursi, Irish moss, ginger, astragalus, capsicum, rose hips and vitamin C*), nourishes depleted adrenal glands. Or, Planetary Formulas SCHIZANDRA ADRENAL SUPPORT, and Herbs Etc. ADRENOTONIC.

To support adrenal glands depleted by stress and hypoglycemic reactions, take B complex 100mg, and Vitamin C 3000-5000mg daily, (or immediately during a sugar drop attack).

•Mucilant herbs are full of fiber that slows sugar absorption to help blood sugar balance. Crystal Star CHO-LO FIBER TONE™ caps (with *oat bran, flax seed, psyllium husks, guar gum, vegetable acidophilus, apple pectin, fennel sd., acerola cherry*), or Nature's Secret ULTIMATE CLEANSE to absorb excess carbohydrates and balance sugar curve.

• To increase oxygen uptake and add minerals, take CoQ-10 60mg and Mezotrace SEA MINERAL COMPLEX daily or Nature's Path TRACE-LYTE liquid minerals in juice.

• To balance sugar use in the bloodstream, take chromium picolinate 200mcg, or Rainbow Light GTF CHROMIUM COMPLEX, or Gaia Herbs DEVIL'S CLUB SUPREME.

• Crystal Star GINSENG 6 SUPER TEA™ (with *prince ginseng, kirin ginseng, echinacea, pau d' arco, suma, astragalus, echinacea, St. John's wort, aralia, ashwagandha, Chinese ginseng, Siberian ginseng, reishi mushroom, fennel, tienchi ginseng*) helps remove sugar from the blood.

• Herbs like *kava, passionflower and scullcap* fight stress reactions linked to hypoglycemia.

You can boost your energy with natural strategies that help diabetes. Overloading on refined carbohydrates, sugary foods and alcohol to relieve chronic stress sets the stage for diabetes, a diseases that robs energy, then heath. Diabetes warning symptoms include: excessive appetite and thirst, and frequent urination. There are two types of diabetes:

Type 1, also known as juvenile-onset, or insulin-dependent diabetes, usually starts in childhood. With this type little or no insulin is produced by the pancreas, and it's thought to be caused by genetic predisposition, injury to the pancreas' insulin-producing beta-cells, and linked to compromised immune status. Diet is important for a Type 1 diabetic's well-being, but since the body doesn't produce insulin, even a good diet must be supplemented with insulin.

Type 2, also known as adult-onset, or non-insulin-dependent diabetes accounts for 90% of all diabetics, and usually occurs later in life, after 40. With this type the pancreas *does* produce insulin, but the body is resistant to it or cannot use it properly. It's thought to be caused by both pancreas and liver malfunction where the body does not metabolize fat and glucose well. This leads to obesity, which itself becomes a compounding problem because it causes loss of insulin sensitivity. Achieving normal body weight can sometimes bring about the restoration of normal blood sugar levels.

Dietary improvement is fundamental to the successful treatment of Type 2 diabetes. While some Type 2 cases must use insulin, many can be controlled by diet alone.

Start with your diet. Diet improvements are simple but absolutely necessary.

Diabetes makes a person want to eat more, and these cravings usually mean eating too much fat, too many sugary foods and carbohydrates of all kinds to fill the body's perceived "energy hole." But as your body loses more ability to manage insulin correctly, less and less simple carbohydrates and sugars are metabolized — they keep accumulating and are stored as fat. The following sugar-balancing diet, in addition to reducing insulin requirements and balancing sugar function in the bloodstream, has the nice "side effect" of healthy weight loss.

Good meals for diabetic sufferers are small, frequent, and largely vegetarian. All sugars, refined, fried and fatty foods are excluded. (High fat, especially saturated fat, is widely associated with diabetes onset.) The key to the diet is slow-burning complex carbohydrate fuels, primarily from vegetables that do not need much insulin for metabolism. Fifty to sixty percent of a good diabetic diet, especially at first, should be fresh or simply cooked vegetables. Slow-release nutrients, like whole grains and legumes prevent rapid blood sugar spikes. Proteins come from soy foods and whole grains rich in lecithin and chromium.

You need to be quite conscious of the foods that affect your sugar balance. It's not just "sugar." ANY foods made with refined flours (like pastries and rolls) are just as bad, or worse, because they clog your insides as well as affect your insulin. Avoid even natural sugars — honey, molasses, maple syrup and alcoholic beverages, until sugar balance is achieved.

1: Include some vegetable protein at every meal — soy foods, beans, brown rice, seafood, sea plants.

2: Include a fresh salad (with flax oil dressing) or green vegetables, or a green supplement drink, like chlorella or spirulina daily for the first month; or Crystal Star ENERGY GREEN™ DRINK (with *rice protein, barley grass and sprouts, alfalfa sprouts, bee pollen, acerola cherry, oat and quinoa sprouts, apple pectin, Siberian ginseng, sarsaparilla, spirulina, chlorella, dandelion, dulse, licorice root, gotu kola, apple juice*). Most people feel the energy results right away.

3: Include high fiber foods, like whole grains and vegetables, to help stabilize sugar swings, improve glucose metabolism, lower cholesterol and triglyceride levels, and promote weight loss. Note: Mucilant herbs, like *psyllium* and *marshmallow* contain fiber that helps to slow the absorption of sugar. Nature's Secret ULTIMATE FIBER, All One WHOLE FIBER COMPLEX.

4: Add cultured foods — raw sauerkraut, yogurt, cottage cheese or kefir for G.I. flora.

5: Chromium helps regulate insulin activity in your body. Lack of chromium plays a role in the sensitivity of cells to insulin. Add chromium-rich foods — whole grains, brewer's yeast, string beans, eggs, cucumbers, soy foods, onions and garlic, shiitake mushrooms, wheat germ.

Herbs and supplements enhance your "sugar strategy" for more energy.

• Pancreatic tonics like *turmeric* caps, and *Siberian ginseng, dandelion/licorice* and *fenugreek seed* tea help normalize high blood sugar. Crystal Star SUGAR STRATEGY HIGH™ CAPS (with *cedar bry., licorice rt., dandelion rt., elecampane, mullein, guar gum, wild yam, uva ursi, kelp, horseradish, bilberry, spirulina, capsicum*) help balance insulin production, especially when the pancreas is exhausted. It helps reduce sugar acid content and mucous waste in the blood, thereby allowing glucose to enter the cells instead of accumulating in the bloodstream.

• Lipoic acid is a powerful antioxidant, important for both body energy and glucose balance. In Europe, lipoic acid has been used for almost 3 decades to treat diabetes. I have used MRI ALPHA-LIPOIC ACID and Source Naturals LIPOIC ACID. Use alpha-lipoic acid with caution and according to directions. It may cause hypoglycemia in some diabetics.

• MSM (methylsulfonylmethane) is an organic sulphur compound widely popular in the natural healing repertoire for anti-aging and arthritis. Sulfur is a component of insulin, the protein hormone secreted by the pancreas essential to carbohydrate metabolism. Lack of dietary sulfur can result in low insulin production. Of special interest to diabetics is the fact that a diet with plenty of organic sulfur may enhance the body's ability to produce insulin to the point at which insulin injections can be reduced. Consider Now or Futurebiotics MSM.

Is your liver dragging your energy down?

The first sign of liver malfunction, congestion or toxicity is unexplained fatigue. Your energy depends on your liver. Here's why:

1: Your liver oversees and manages all the nutrients you take in. It's the primary metabolic organ for proteins, fats and carbohydrates. For example, if the blood contains too high a level of amino acids (after eating), the liver converts some of them into glucose, some into proteins, some into other amino acids and some into urea (passed to the kidneys for excretion).

2: Your liver also *produces* nutrients from blood plasma — special proteins and cholesterol. It synthesizes and secretes bile, a substance that insures good food assimilation and is critical to the excretion of toxic material from the gastrointestinal tract.

3: Your liver is the primary organ that processes metabolic and environmental toxins to protect your body from harm. It filters out toxins at a rate of approximately a quart of blood per minute and at any given time contains approximately 20 percent of the body's blood.

Still, the liver is a remarkably resilient organ. Seventy-five percent of its cells can be destroyed before it ceases to function. Health problems usually only occur after many years of overtaxing, when the liver becomes so exhausted it loses the ability to detoxify itself.

You can help your liver take a "deep cleansing breath"... something I've found you can almost feel as its miraculous powers of recovery begin to flow.

Check out the following liver exhaustion symptom list. You may need to re-energize your liver so your liver can re-energize you.
- Have you been drinking alot of alcohol lately?
- Are you taking several rounds of prescription drugs, like antibiotics and tranquilizers?
- Do you eat foods with preservatives, stabilizers, chemical flavors and colors, or hormone injections (meats and dairy products)?
- Do you live in an environment with noticeable air pollution or chemical exposure?
- Is your diet high in refined sugar and carbohydrates, and fast foods?
- Do you eat few vegetables and little daily fiber?
- Have you been under long term emotional or mental stress, or depression?
- Do you have chronic insomnia, headaches, muscle aches and stiffness, or skin disorders?
- Do you have high cholesterol and related problems, like gallstones or high blood pressure?

Here are some of the highlights from my complete "Liver Health" program in *Healthy Healing*, and "Liver Cleansing" in *Detoxification* to jump start your liver revitalization program.

Start with a short cleansing diet:

Your liver responds to cleansing assistance more rapidly than any other organ. Relieve your liver of toxic build-up by eliminating commercial red meats (antibiotic and hormone injections), fried and sugary foods, and clogging, partially hydrogenated fats and oils. Avoid alcohol during your cleanse. Choose organically grown produce, hormone and chemical free meats and dairy for the best results. Eat high quality *vegetable proteins*, rather than meats for at least a month. Vegetable fiber foods absorb excess bile and increase regularity for cleansing. Eat plenty of fresh vegetables and fruits for plant enzymes.

Follow the cleanse for 3 to 4 days. Then follow a diet of 100% fresh foods for the rest of the week. Add $1/4$ tsp. Vitamin C crystals to each drink you take. It's a natural chelator of heavy metal toxins that deteriorate liver function. Don't forget — 8 glasses of water throughout the day.

The night before your liver cleanse.....
—Take a cup of miso soup with sea veggies snipped on top.
The next day....
—On rising: take 2 TBS. cider vinegar in water with 1 tsp. honey, or Crystal Star GREEN TEA CLEANSER™ tea (with *green tea, burdock, gotu kola, fo-ti, hawthorn, orange peel, cinnamon*).
—Breakfast: take a glass of potassium juice (carrot, spinach, parsley, celery), or Crystal Star SYSTEMS STRENGTH DRINK™ (with nutrients from *alfalfa, borage, yellow dock, oatstraw, dandelion, barley grass, licorice, watercress, pau d'arco, nettles, horsetail, red raspberry, fennel, parsley, bilberry, Siberian ginseng rt., schizandra, rosemary, dulse, wakame, kombu, sea palm, miso, soy, cranberry, and nutritional yeast*). Add 1 teasp. spirulina powder to either drink.
—Mid-morning: take a green superfood powder in water or vegetable juice (Some choices: Green Foods GREEN MAGMA, Crystal Star ENERGY GREEN™ -*page 87,* or NutriCology PRO-GREENS).
—Lunch: have a glass of fresh carrot juice or a glass of organic apple juice.
—Mid-afternoon: have a cup of peppermint tea, or Crystal Star LIV-ALIVE TEA™ (with *dandelion, watercress, yellow dock, pau d'arco bk., hyssop, parsley, Oregon grape, sage, licorice, milk thistle sd., hibiscus);* or another green drink.
—Dinner: have another carrot juice or a mixed vegetable juice; or have a hot vegetable broth.
—Before Bed: take another glass of lemon juice or cider vinegar in water. Add 1 tsp. honey or royal jelly; or a pineapple/papaya juice with 1 tsp. royal jelly.

Liver super green foods to consider for the rest of your liver restoration program:
• Crystal Star ENERGY GREEN™, Etherium LIFESOURCE, Body Ecology VITALITY SUPERGREEN, Wakunaga of America KYO-GREEN, Transformation Enzyme SUPER CELLZYME caps, Nature's Secret ULTIMATE GREEN.

Herbal combinations are good long term liver support. Take for 3 to 6 months after your cleanse.
• *Milk thistle seed* - research shows milk thistle accelerates liver regeneration by a factor of four. Nature's Apothecary or Crystal Star MILK THISTLE SEED EXTRACT; Enzymatic Therapy SUPER MILK THISTLE COMPLEX WITH ARTICHOKE; Nutrition Now DANDELION & MILK THISTLE EXTRACT.

• Bitters herbs stimulate the liver and bile flow: Crystal Star BITTERS & LEMON CLEANSER™; Floradix HERBAL BITTERS; Herbs Etc. LIVER TONIC; Solaray *turmeric* caps; *dandelion* root and leaf tea.

• Alterative (blood cleansing) herbs, like *echinacea, burdock, garlic, red clover, sarsaparilla, goldenseal, nettles and yellow dock* strengthen your liver, restore vitality and blood composition.

• Lipoic acid is among the most powerful liver detoxifiers ever discovered. Among its advocates: Dr. Fred Barter, M.D., Ph.D. for over 19 years has used lipoic acid for 20 years in over 100 patients with sudden liver failure. In the 1970s, he treated two terminally ill patients with amanita poisoning, one of the deadliest poisons in nature. He cured the patients with 800mg, administered in four infusions of 200mg. Amazingly, the lipoic acid reversed the liver damage in both patients and they lived. MRI ALPHA-LIPOIC ACID; Source Naturals LIPOIC ACID.

• Lipotropics prevent fatty accumulation: Phosphatidyl choline, choline 600mg, or Solaray LIPOTROPIC PLUS; sea vegetables (any kind) every day; *dandelion* tea; *gotu kola* or *fennel seed* tea.

Once you get rid of your energy sappers, you can bring in energy boosters.

Start with the foundation — energizing stored in its molecular bonds. Releasing the and into your cells is known as energy trans- transferred to adenosine triphosphate (ATP), body. ATP is especially involved in our body break down the food molecules to make en- of foods supplies your body with the wealth food. Food has chemical energy chemical energy from these bonds fer. The chemical energy in food is a special energy carrier molecule in the energy factories—the mitochondria, which ergy available to our bodies. A wide variety of Nature's natural energy stores.

Here are some of power foods I count on for long lasting energy:

—**Apples and Berries** - contain pectin which releases clusters of fatigue-causing fat.

—**Asparagus** - contains asparagine, an alkaloid that breaks down fat accumulations.

—**Bananas** - contain potassium, vitamin B-6, and biotin which sweep away fatty deposits.

—**Barley** - contains complex carbohydrates for energy; also helps rid the body of wastes that drain energy; rich in chlorophyll that neutralizes toxins to improve body chemistry.

—**Beans** - contain energizing complex carbohydrates which give sustained energy.

—**Beets** - contain a form of low-level iron that cleanses blood cells and flushes away fatty deposits. They are rich in minerals which wash fats from your liver, kidney, and gall bladder.

—**Brown rice** - an excellent source of the B-complex vitamins which spark energy.

—**Cabbage** - fatigue-causing wastes are flushed by the sulfur and iron in cabbage.

—**Carrots** - activate metabolism, energize cells and promotes fat-flushing action.

—**Celery** - calcium riches energize the endocrine system, producing hormones which break down fatty build-up in cells. Celery's magnesium and iron nourish the blood. Its natural sodium flushes inorganic mineral wastes, such as those that occur in arthritis.

—**Chili peppers** - contain capsaicin which thins toxic wastes that clog breathing passages, promoting more oxygen for your system activities. Chilies also boost metabolic rate.

—**Citrus fruits** - their vitamin C reduces the sluggishness of fat.

—**Figs** - rich in complex carbohydrates that enter the bloodstream quickly and provide an energy surge. They also provide many vitamins and minerals which add to the energy equation.

—**Garlic** - contains allicin to revitalize metabolism, boost energy and enhance immunity.

—**Kale and cruciferous vegetables** - contain indole-3-carbinol which quickens metabolism and boosts energy. Also contain absorbable calcium which balances energy hormones.

—**Peas** - rich in potassium and magnesium — energizing gland tonics.

—**Peppers** - contain vitamin C and beta-carotene to sustain energy.

—**Soybeans** - contain lecithin which releases a substance called lecithin cholesterol acyltransferase (LCAT). LCAT breaks down fatty deposits and flushes them out of the body.

—**Spices** - cinnamon, cloves and turmeric — help balance blood sugar by improving the effectiveness of insulin production, thus giving sustained energy.

—**Tomatoes** - contain vitamin C and natural citric acids which invigorate metabolic processes, and fatty deposits are filtered out of the bloodstream by enzyme-activated minerals.

—**Wheat germ** - contains energizing B-complex vitamins for physical and liver support.

What about energy stimulants?

Most Americans today feel they need more energy to meet the increased demands on their time and responsibilities. We're taking energy stimulants of all kinds, mental and physical, natural and synthetic to keep fatigue at bay. But do most of them do more harm than good? Do they end up sapping your energy rather than returning it?

Are the energy stimulants available today safe?

Stimulants increase a system function or a metabolic action to create a sense of well-being, exhilaration and self-confidence, or relieve fatigue and drowsiness. Many stimulants, however, especially chemical blends, breed tolerance, dependency, lethargy, irritability, nervousness, and restlessness. Many chemical stimulants draw in so much "energy," your body can't use it all — you'll have trouble concentrating, feel shaky and get after-effect headaches. Americans often live by the principle that "if a little is good, more is better," but stronger stimulants may increase their toxicity or dependency potential. Taken too often, stimulants, even some natural ones can drive a body system to exhaustion.

Natural energizers have great advantages over chemical stimulants.

Most natural stimulants, such as those from whole herbs, have broader based activity so that they don't exhaust an organ or body system. They can be strong or gentle for individual needs without the downside of depleting the body's energy stores or overwhelming body systems. Normally they work through the body's own processes as nutrient support rather than by drawing off energy stores.

Natural energizers fall into three general classes: central nervous system stimulants, metabolic enhancers and adaptogens. **Which are the best energizers, and how should they be used for the best effects?**

Central Nervous System Stimulants

CNS stimulants affect the cerebral cortex and the medulla of the brain. Most contain either natural caffeine, naturally-occurring ephedrine, or some of the free-form amino acids. In general, these substances promote alertness, energy, and a more rapid, clearer flow of thought. They also act as respiratory stimulants. I find most central nervous system stimulants should be used for short term needs. Most people find that long term use can result in a net loss of energy to the body. Seriously limit or avoid central nervous system stimulants during pregnancy.

•**Caffeine** is America's most popular stimulant. There is solid evidence for caffeine's positive effects on mental performance and shortened reaction times. Caffeine stimulates serotonin, a brain neurotransmitter. It increases the capacity for intellectual tasks, and decreases drowsiness. In moderate doses, caffeine improves mood and increases alertness by releasing adrenaline into the bloodstream. It mobilizes essential fatty acids into the circulatory system facilitating energy production, endurance and work output. It has a direct potentiating effect on muscle contraction for sports activities. Caffeine also has analgesic properties. Taking aspirin or an herbal pain reliever with a caffeine drink increases pain relieving effects.

• **Guaraña** - A rich, natural source of the rainforest xanthine, guaranine, it provides long, slow endurance energy without the health problems posed by coffee's heated hydrocarbons.

• **Kola nut** - A rich, natural source of caffeine, also without heated hydrocarbons, from Africa. It allays hunger and combats fatigue. It is often used in herbal energy products.

• **Tyrosine** - A rapidly metabolized amino acid and effective source of quick energy for the brain. Tyrosine builds adrenalin and thyroid stores. It is a safe energizer in cases of depression, is useful in controlling drug abuse and aiding drug withdrawal. Increases libido and low sex drive.

• **L-Phenylalanine** - A tyrosine precursor that works through the central nervous system with vitamin B-6 as an anti-depressant and mood elevator. It must be avoided by those who are phenalketonuric (PK).

• **Glutamine** - An amino acid that converts readily into 6-carbon glucose as an effective energy source for the brain. It rapidly improves memory retention, concentration and alertness.

• **Yerba Maté** - A South American stimulant herb that naturally diminishes stress fatigue, maté is a rejuvenating xanthine-type energizer without caffeine.

• **Ephedra** - A long lasting CNS stimulant that calms the mind as it stimulates the body. Although it contains the potent isolates ephedrine and pseudo-ephedrine, ephedra in its whole form is a superior bronchodilator and decongestant, and an energy tonic that increases metabolism. As a cardiac stimulant, ephedra is not advised for anyone with high blood pressure.

• **Ginkgo Biloba** - A primary brain and mental energy stimulant, ginkgo increases both peripheral and cerebral circulation through vasodilation. It is an excellent choice as a stimulant for the elderly with poor memory and other aging-related CNS problems. Ginkgo increases acetylcholine levels stimulating the body to better transmit electrical impulses. Ginkgo also improves oxygen delivery to the cells of the body — important for energy endurance.

• **Yohimbe** - A hormone stimulant, effective in increasing testosterone production. Because of this quality, it has an aphrodisiac effect — primarily on a deficient male system. Yohimbe should be avoided if you have high blood pressure or heart arrythmia.

Natural food store products that stimulate CNS energy:
• Crystal Star High Performance™ Caps
• Crystal Star High Energy Tea
• Crystal Star Rainforest Energy™ Caps
• Rainbow Light Ginkgo Supercomplex, Naturade Ginkgo
• Rainbow Light Ultra Energy Plus, Futurebiotics Living Energy
• Wisdom Of The Ancients Yerba Mate, Medicine Wheel Memory Booster
• Enzymatic Therapy Thyroid & L-Tyrosine Complex

Metabolic Enhancers

Metabolic enhancers improve the performance of your body's biochemical pathways by providing catalysts and support co-factors. Metabolic enhancers help your body produce more energy, largely through micro-nutrient use (vitamins) and enzyme reactions. Examples of metabolic enhancers include co-enzyme factors like B vitamins, energy potentiators like minerals, fat mobilizers like carnitine, electron transporters like CoQ-10, and tissue oxygenators like DMG.

1: Enzyme energizers: your body's metabolic enzymes and co-enzymes carry an energy factor needed for every chemical action for all your 100 *trillion* cells. • Metabolic enzymes enable us to *capture energy* from food. Food contains thermodynamic energy; enzymes release the energy. • Enzymes also *carry energy* throughout the body to do their work.

2: CoQ-10: an essential catalyst electron transporter for cellular energy in the body. The body's ability to assimilate food source CoQ-10 declines with age. Supplementation provides wide ranging therapeutic benefits for every body system.

3: Carnitine: a non-essential amino acid, carnitine is largely synthesized by the liver from lysine, methionine and vitamin C and found in animal muscle and organ meats (hence its name "carni-tine"). Carnitine is essential in the metabolism of fats. With the ability to transfer fatty acids across mitochondria membranes, carnitine makes fatty acids usable as sources of energy. In essence, carnitine helps our bodies harvest the energy from the fats we eat.

4: B-Complex vitamins: are essential for metabolism, the body's energy transfer process. B-vitamins are water-soluble. Your body isn't able to store them long. You need to keep a continuous supply coming in for energy. Foods rich in the B-vitamins include nutritional yeast, brown rice, wheat germ and seafoods. Adding a good B-Complex supplement is a good idea.

—DMG, Di-Methyl-Glycine, commonly known as B15, is a powerful antioxidant and energy stimulant whose effects are attributed to its conversion to glycine.

—Bee pollen and royal jelly are rich sources of B-complex vitamins, especially pantothenic acid which combats stress, and supplies key nutrients for energy and mental alertness.

5: Metabolic minerals: don't directly supply energy, but rather function instead through the body's metabolism to produce energy. Magnesium, potassium, chromium, and zinc all influence energy through their regulation of insulin metabolism and glucose use. Iron transports oxygen in the blood to muscles, organs and body tissue.

Natural food store products that enhance metabolic energy:
• Transformation Super Cellzyme, Rainbow Light Advanced Enzyme System
• Herbal Products and Development Power-Plus Food Enzymes
• Country Life Coenzyme B-Complex, L-Carnitine & B-6
• Nature's Secret Ultimate B
• Source Naturals Dibencozide Sublingual, Vitamin B12 Sublingual
• Nature's Path Trace-Lyte, Trace Minerals Research Concentrace
• NutriCology CoQ10 With Tocotrienols, Rainbow Light CoQ10 System

Adaptogens

Adaptogens are body chemistry regulators that help you handle stress and maintain vitality. They increase the body's overall immune function with broad spectrum activity, rather than specific action. I use them regularly for their synergistic action with other herbs. Adaptogens give every herbal formula "energy." They are rich sources of important strength nutrients like germanium and steroid-like compounds especially important in restoring the endocrine, nervous, digestive, muscle and the liver. They may be used for for long term revitalization to restore body balance as well as more immediate energy.

One of the most significant features of herbal adaptogens is that they supply energy to your body by *normalizing* rather than over-stimulating. They don't interfere with the regular function of your body systems or organs. They are true tonics, not energy sappers.

Adaptogens that make a real difference in the energy you feel:

• **Panax Ginseng:** the most effective adaptogen herb, ginseng stimulates both long and short-term energy, promotes regeneration from stress and fatigue, rebuilds foundation strength and has measurable amounts of germanium (a potent adaptogen mineral in its own right).

• **Siberian Ginseng:** (*eleuthero*) is a long-term tonic that supports the adrenal glands, the circulatory system, stamina and endurance, and immune response. It stimulates the brain to improve concentration.

Note: Numerous studies show both ginsengs above exert significant anti-anxiety effects. The stress-relieving effects are found to be comparable to those of diazepam (Valium). Clinical research shows that Chinese (*panax*) and Siberian ginseng can: enhance the body's ability to respond to stress; increase physical and mental performance; increase energy and restore vitality; offset some negative effects of cortisone; enhance liver function; protect against radiation damage; and produce a sense of well-being.

• **Astragalus:** a superior tonic and strong immune-enhancing herb, astragalus nourishes exhausted adrenals to combat fatigue. Astragalus provides therapeutic support for recovery from illness or surgery, especially from chemotherapy and radiation.

• **Suma:** a rainforest energizer with ginseng-like properties has been found to be as effective as the illegal synthetic steroid, dianabol, without the side effects. Widely popular with American body builders, its active steroid, beta-ecdysterone helps the body utilize protein for energy.

Natural food store products with effective adaptogens:
• Crystal Star GINSENG SIX™
• Nature's Secret ULTIMATE ENERGY
• Medicine Wheel FOUNTAIN OF YOUTH
• Rainbow Light ADAPTOGEM
• Planetary Formulas ELIXIR OF LIFE
• Rainbow Light TEN GINSENGS SUPERCOMPLEX
• Hsu's Ginseng Enterprises WILD AMERICAN GINSENG

Bibliography

Page, Linda R. *Healthy Healing* - Tenth Edition. 1997

Page, Linda R. *Detoxification - All you need to know to recharge, renew and rejuvenate your body.* 1999

Page, Linda R. *How To Be Your Own Herbal Pharmacist.* 1997

Page, Linda R. *Stress Management Depression.* 1995

Page, Linda R. *The Energy Crunch & You.* 1993

Gilbert, M., M.S., C.H.E.S., L.M.T. "Managing Stress, Pathways to Adaptation and Balance," *NSN.* Sept. 1998

Hobbs, Christopher, L.Ac. *Stress & Natural Healing.* 1997

Murray, Michael, N.D. and Joseph Pizzorno, N.D. *Encyclopedia of Natural Medicine.* 1998

Langer, Stephen, M.D., "Break The Chain - Control Stress With Nutrition," *Better Nutrition.* Dec. 1997

Childre, Doc Lew. *Fast Action Stress Relief - Freeze Frame.* 1994

Dunne, Lavon J. *Nutrition Almanac.* 1990

Balch, James F., M.D. and Phyllis A. Balch, C.N.C. *Prescription for Nutritional Healing.* 1997

Castleman, Michael. "37 Ways to Peace of Mind," *American Health.* April 1998

Wallace, Edward C., N.D., D.C. "Adaptogenic Herbs: Nature's Solution To Stress," *Nutr. Science.* May 1998

Werbach, Melvyn R., M.D. *Nutritional Influences on Illness - A Sourcebook of Clinical Research.* 1988.

Pitchford, Paul. *Healing with Whole Foods - Oriental Traditions and Modern Nutrition.* 1993

Slagle, Priscilla, M.D. *The Way Up From Down - Rid Yourself of: Stress, Low Moods, Depression.* 1992.

Baumel, Syd. *Dealing With Depression Naturally.* 1995

Lombard, Dr. Jay, Neurologist and Carl Germano, R.D., C.N.S., L.D.N. *The Brain Wellness Plan.* 1997

Khalsa, Karta Purkh Singh, C.N., A.H.G. "Boost Your Brain Power With Ginkgo," *Let's Live.* January 1998

Ethridge, Esther. "Brain Food," *Energy Times.* October 1997

Gagnon, Daniel, "St. John's Wort Provides an Herbal Alternative to Prozac," *The Santa Fe Sun.* June 1997

Murray, Michael T., N.D. *Natural Alternatives to Prozac.* 1996

Levine, Stephen, Ph. D., Parris M. Kidd, Ph.D. *Antioxidant Adaptation - Its Role in Free Radical Pathology.* 1994

Friedrich, Joan, Ph.D. "Understanding And Coping With Stress," *Let's Live.* August 1993

Robertson, Jane L. "Breathe Your Way to Health and Happiness," *Body Mind Spirit.* May/June 1994

Mindell, Earl L., R.Ph., Ph.D. *The MSM Miracle - Enhance your health with organic sulfur.* 1997

Cichoke, Dr. Anthony J., *The Complete Book Of Enzyme Therapy,* 1999

Tunella, Kim, C.D.C. "Some of the Problems of Chronically Low Blood Sugar," 1995

Powell, J. Robin, Ph.D., CSW, Holly George-Warren. *The Working Women's Guide to Managing Stress.* 1994

Aesoph, Lauri M., N.D. *How To Eat Away Arthritis.* 1996

Theodosakis, Jason, M.D., M.S.,M.P.H., et al. *The Arthritis Cure.* 1997

Steinman, David. "Enter The Energy Zone," *Delicious.* March 1997

Freedom, David, and Tierra True, *Nature's Path To Supreme Health,* 1998

Aesoph, Lauri M., N.D. "Nutrients That Energize," *Nutrition Science News.* February 1998

Becker, Robert O., M.D. and Gary Selden. *The Body Electric - Electromagnetism and The Foundation of Life.* 1985

Sugarman, Ellen, Warning: *The Electricity Around You May Be Hazardous To Your Health.* 1998

Bragg, Patrica, N.D., Ph.D. and Paul C. Bragg, N.D., Ph.D. *Super Power Breathing For Super Energy.* 1999

Mowrey, Daniel B., Ph.D. "Energy Vitamins," *Energy Times.* June 1998

Stress & Energy Product Resources

The following list is for your convenience in obtaining small company products recommended in this book. We look for the most effective products for each particular problem. The list is unsolicited by the companies named.

If you can't find a product, call the Healthy House @ 888-447-2939.

- Aloe Life International, 4822 Santa Monica Ave. #231, San Diego, CA 92107, 800-414-2563
- Alta Health Products, Inc., 1979 E. Locust Street, Pasadena, CA 91107, 626-796-1047
- America's Finest, Inc., 140 Ethel Road West, Suites S & T, Piscataway, NJ 08854, 800-350-3305
- American Health & Herbs, P.O. Box 94 - 1313 Main Street, Philomath, OR 97370, 800-345-4152
- Arise & Shine, P.O. Box 1439, Mt. Shasta, CA 96067, 800-688-2444
- Beehive Botanicals, Route 8, Box 8257, Hayward, WI 54843, 800-233-4483
- Bio-Tech Foods Ltd., 250 S. Hotel St., Ste. 200, Honolulu, HI 96813-2869, 800-468-7578
- Body Ecology, 6515 Aldrich Road, Bellingham, WA 98226, 800-511-2660
- Boericke & Tafel Inc., 2381 Circadian Way, Santa Rosa, CA 95407, 800-876-9505
- Burt's Bees, 2050 Greenway Ave., Charlotte, NC 28204, 704-370-6671
- Country Life, 28300 B Industrial Blvd., Hayward, CA 94545, 510-785-1196
- Crystal Star Herbal Nutrition, 6305 Wedgeway Ct., Earth City, MO, 63045, 800-736-6015
- Diamond/Herpanacine Associates,138 Stout Rd., P.O. Box 544, Ambler, PA 19002, 215-542-2981
- Eidon Silica Products, 9988, Hibert St. #104, San Diego, CA 92131, 800-700-1169
- EtheriumTechnology, Inc., 16004 SW Tualatin-Sherwood Rd., Suite 503, Sherwood, OR 97140, 503-625-2880
- Flora, Inc., 805 East Badger Road, P.O. Box 73, Lynden, WA 98264, 800-446-2110, (Info.) 604-451-8232
- Gaia Herbs, Inc., 12 Lancaster County Road, Harvard, MA 01451, 800-831-7780
- Golden Pride, 1501 Northpoint Pkwy., Suite 100, West Palm Beach, FL 33407, 561-640-5700
- Green Foods Corp., 320 North Graves Ave., Oxnard, CA 93030, 800-777-4430
- Green Kamut Corp., 1542 Seabright Ave., Long Beach, CA 90813, 800-452-6884
- Healthy Tek, Inc., 2502 S. Broadway, Yorktown, IN 47396, 800-937-1104
- Heart Foods Company, Inc., 2235 East 38th Street, Minneapolis, MN 55407, 612-724-5266
- Herbal Answers, Inc. P.O. Box 1110, Saratoga Springs, NY 12866, 888-256-3367
- Herbal Products & Development, P.O. Box 1084, Aptos, CA 95001, 831-688-8706
- Herbs Etc., 1340 Rufina Circle, Santa Fe, NM 87505, 505-471-6488
- Institute of HeartMath, P.O. 1463, 14700 West Park Ave., Boulder Creek, CA 95006, 800-450-9111
- Live Food Products, Inc. Box 7, Santa Barbara, CA 93102, 800-446-1990
- Living Light Energies, 31-130 Cedar St. Suite 424, Cambridge, Ontario, Canada, N1S 5A5, 888-349-3553
- Maine Coast Sea Vegetables, RR1 Box 78, Franklin, Maine 04634, 207-565-2907
- Matrix Health Products, 8400 Magnolia Ave., Ste. N, Santee, CA 92071, 800-736-5609
- Mendocino Sea Vegetable Co., P.O. Box 1265, Mendocino, CA 95460, 707-937-2050
- Motherlove Herbal Co., P.O. Box 101, Laporte, CO 80535, 970-493-2892
- National Enzyme Company, Hwy. 160, P.O. Box 128, Forsyth, MO 65653, 800-825-8545
- Natural Labs Corp. (Deva Flowers), P.O. Box 20037, Sedona, AZ 86341-0037, 800-233-0810
- Nature's Answer, 320 Oser Avenue, Hauppauge, NY 11788, 800-439-2324
- Nature's Path, P.O. Box 7862, Venice, FL 34287, 800-326-5772
- Nature's Secret/Irwin Naturals, 10549 West Jefferson Blvd., Culver City, CA 90232, 310-253-5305
- Nonie of Beverly Hills, Inc. 16158 Wyancotte Street, Vans Nuys, CA 91406, 310-271-7988
- NOW, 395 S. Glen Ellyn Rd., Bloomingdale, IL 60108, 800-999-8069
- NutriCology, 30806 Santana Street, Hayward, CA 94544, 800-545-9960 / 510-487-8526
- Professional Nutrition, 811 Cliff Dr. , Suite C-1, Santa Barbara, CA 93109, 800-336-9301
- Prozyme Products, LTD., 6600 N. Lincoln Ave., Suite 312, Lincolnwood, IL. 60645, 800-522-5537
- Rainbow Light, P.O. Box 600, Santa Cruz, CA 95061, 800-635-1233
- Rejuvenative Foods, P.O. Box 8464, Santa Cruz, CA 95061, 800-805-7957
- Sage Associates, 1225 Coast Village Road, Suite G, Santa Barbara, CA 93108, 805-969-0557
- Sage Woman Herbs Ltd., 2211 W. Colorado Ave., Colorado Springs, CO 80904, 719-473-9702
- Sonne's Organic Foods, Inc., P.O.Box 2160, Cottonwood, CA 96022, 800-544-8147
- Source Naturals Inc. 23 Janis Way, Scotts Valley, CA 95066, 800-777-5677
- Springlife Inc., 4630 N. Paseo Delos Cerritos, Tucson, AZ 85745, 888-633-9233
- Transformation Enzyme Corporation, 2900 Wilcrest, Suite 220, Houston, TX, 77042, 800-777-1474
- Waddell Creek Organic Bee Pollen, 654 Swanton Road, Davenport, CA 95017
- Wakunaga of America Co., Ltd., 23501 Madero, Mission Viejo, CA 92691-2764, 800-421-2998 / 800-825-7888
- Wyndmere Naturals, Inc., 153 Ashley Road, Hopkins, MN 55343, 800-207-8538
- Y.S. Royal Jelly & Organic Bee Farm, RT. 1, Box 91-A, Sheridan IL 60551, 800-654-4593